the new southwest cookbook

the new southwest cookbook

Carolyn Niethammer

RIO NUEVO PUBLISHERS
TUCSON, ARIZONA

Rio Nuevo Publishers®

P.O. Box 5250, Tucson, Arizona 85703-0250

(520) 623-9558, www.rionuevo.com

Tortilla Lasagna, Corn Risotto, and Terra Cotta Salsa Fresca are reprinted from *Contemporary Southwest, The
Café Terra Cotta Cookbook,* by Donna Nordin, published by Ten Speed Press, 2000. Chile con Queso and
Tostadas Compuestas are reprinted from *The Authentic La Posta Cookbook,* by Kathy Camuñez, published by La
Posta, 1971. Pumpkin Flan and Sopaipillas are reprinted from *The Rancho de Chimayo Cookbook,* by Cheryl
Jamison, published by Harvard Common Press, 1991. Rosalita, Steak Dunigan, and Gypsy Stew are reprinted from
The Pink Adobe Cookbook, by Rosalea Murphy, published by Dell, 1988. Spiced Artichokes are reprinted from
With A Measure of Grace, by Blake Spaulding, Jennifer Castle, and Lavinia Spaulding, published by Provecho
Press, 2004. All recipes used with permission.

Library of Congress Cataloging-in-Publication Data

Niethammer, Carolyn J.
The new Southwest cookbook / Carolyn Niethammer.
    p. cm.
Includes index.
ISBN-13: 978-1-887896-78-8 (pbk.)
ISBN-10: 1-887896-78-3 (pbk.)
1. Cookery, American--Southwestern style. I. Title.

TX715.2.S69N56 2005
641.5979--dc22

2005017067

On the front cover: Blackened Shrimp with Tomatillo Sauce (photo by Robin
Stancliff, food styling by Tracy Vega). Landscape photo on front and back
covers by George Stocking.

Design: Karen Schober
Illustrations: Kate Quinby

Printed in Canada.

10 9 8 7 6 5 4 3 2 1

ACKNOWLEDGMENTS

. . . .

Thank you to all the busy chefs at some of the Southwest's most outstanding restaurants for taking the time to restructure their innovative recipes for home cooks and for answering my numerous follow-up questions. Martha Blue, Zeke Browning, Ginia Desmond, Elisabeth Ruffner, Sarah Dinham, and Rosemerry Trommer helped lead me to great Southwestern chefs. Tom Niethammer, Marci Wrenn, and Patricia Wagner, all excellent cooks, helped with recipe testing. Many friends came to dinner or accepted the offer of dessert or salad at their dinner parties as I was doing the recipe testing. Sometimes my husband, Ford Burkhart, ate recipe tests for all three meals in a day! All projects of this complexity are a team project. Editors Lisa Cooper and Kate Rogers did a heroic job of making sure all the recipes were complete in every nuance.

Hostessing experts advise that you should never try a brand-new recipe on company, but I cooked most of these dishes for the first time for neighbors or friends—and the food did not disappoint. Here's to creating your own fabulous meals to share with the people you most like to gather around your table.

contents

introduction:
just what *is* southwest cuisine?

Southwest cooking has always been full of bold, strong flavors and brilliant colors. Plates sport bright red and green chile sauces, yellow pumpkin and other squashes, even blue corn. Inspiration has come from Native American, Mexican, and Spanish cuisines, and recipes have been adapted from the various European traditions of Anglo immigrants to the area.

To truly understand what constitutes cooking in the "new" Southwest, as well as its evolution, we need to first consider the "old" Southwest. For this book that region is defined as the deserts and mountains of West Texas, New Mexico, and Arizona, the canyonlands of southern Colorado and southern Utah, and the extreme desert areas of southeastern California.

For three thousand years, corn, squash, and beans—the so-called Three Sisters— were the basis of the indigenous inhabitants' diets. These foods were augmented by wild greens and seeds, mesquite pods, cactus pads and cactus fruits, and wild game. What made it all palatable, at least to local tastes, was chile. Ignaz Pffeferkorn, a German Jesuit priest and naturalist who traveled through northern Mexico and other parts of New Spain in the mid-1700s, wrote of chile, "They ... eat it with such appetite that their mouths froth and tears come to their eyes. They are fonder of this food than we are of the finest garden lettuce." He then gave a method for preparing chile sauce with meat and concluded, "No dish is more agreeable to an American, but to a foreigner it is intolerable."

About this time, Spanish missionaries and settlers had arrived and began to expand the range of foods available in the area, bringing wheat, pigs, chickens and their eggs, cattle and milk, and fruits such as citrus and grapes. The rise of cattle ranching throughout the Southwest made beef—whether thick steaks grilled over coals or fatty chunks stirred into spicy stews—nearly ubiquitous at the dinner table. People of means with gardens and well-managed homesteads could eat well at home, but meals in commercial establishments remained primitive.

If you were lucky, a top-quality meal served in an overland stagecoach station included dried beef, pinto beans, corn bread or tortillas, and black coffee. Frequently, however, it was merely undercooked beans, chile sauce, and coffee. When the railroad finally traversed southern Arizona and New Mexico in 1880 and 1881, things improved considerably. Fresh fruits and vegetables and seafood arrived packed in ice from California's coast. Restaurants in Tombstone featured elaborate menus, and the *New York Times* reported that the little mining town sported the best eating establishments between St. Louis and San Francisco. But when the mines played out and the wealth disappeared, the fancy restaurants closed.

For the next hundred years, inventive home cooks continued to present their families with great food, but restaurants in the Southwest were mostly limited to American steak and fish houses, standard Mexican enchilada-taco-burrito affairs, and the occasional Italian or Chinese place.

Then in the mid-1980s, the restaurant world in the Southwest began to see an explosion of creativity. Jaime West, executive chef at Westward Look Resort in Tucson, believes that the growth of what we now call Southwest Cuisine was a part of the heightened interest in American cuisine in general. Whereas previously chefs had looked to Europe—mainly France and Italy—for inspiration, they now began to appreciate our regional specialties, including homegrown ingredients and techniques. California, with the influence of Alice Waters, led the way in regional cuisine. Southwest cooks capitalized on that, adding an emphasis on corn, chiles, and other traditional spices.

In the past few decades, the pace of our burgeoning cuisine has not slowed, but in fact accelerated. New restaurants open, bringing in professionally educated chefs who get inspired by the local ingredients and culture. Trained in the intricate art of sauces and reductions and the layering of flavors through complex seasonings, these chefs love the earthy flavors of corn, beans, and squash, but give them endless new twists. They also bring ingredients with them that are often wholly new to the area but enhance our traditional favorites. These new-breed chefs were and are a hit.

Encouraged by the enthusiasm of diners here for their creations, chefs let their imaginations soar. According to Scottsdale chef Robert McGrath, frequently a national spokesman for the area cuisine, "The Southwest region is typified by a boldness of spirit and the ability to pioneer new directions. It only makes sense that the cuisine of the Southwest personifies these characteristics—food that reflects the integrity of the balance of nature and that is also fun to prepare and fun to eat."

The sense of balance McGrath refers to has led many Southwestern chefs to include locally grown and sustainably produced products on their menus. Xanterra Parks and Resorts, which operates lodges in national parks including Grand Canyon,

Bryce, Zion, and Death Valley, emphasizes sustainable cuisine whenever possible. Among the products they use are Fair Trade coffee, wild salmon, and organic wines. Tim Stein, director of food and beverage for Xanterra, says, "From the beginning, our goal has been to educate our guests and employees about the importance of making environmentally responsible cuisine decisions."

At Westward Look Resort in Tucson, citrus is harvested from the many trees on the property, and herbs are grown in the Chef's Garden. Lon's at the Hermosa in Paradise Valley, Arizona, uses meat from Navajo Churro sheep in their lamb dishes, while Tall Timber Resort outside of Durango features a traditional strain of legumes called Anasazi beans in an appetizer.

To let home cooks try their hand at some of these exciting new creations, we invited the Southwest's top restaurant and resort chefs to submit their favorite recipes.

Fusion-style food—the bringing together of ingredients and methods from different cultures—has been a popular American restaurant trend for many years, and a fusion of the Mexican, Indian, and Anglo traditions has been happening in the Southwest for a century. But today's version of fusion cuisine reaches out even further— across continents, even oceans. It is a trial-and-error concept, and some of what fusion has produced is downright awful! But the chefs we feature here have carried out the challenge brilliantly.

John Nobil of El Tovar Lodge at the Grand Canyon adds fresh wild salmon from the Pacific Northwest to a tostada dressed with hot chile oil and a side of Fire-Roasted Corn Salsa. At the Inn of the Anasazi in Santa Fe, mashed potatoes come with cheddar cheese and chipotle chiles. At Furnace Creek Inn in Death Valley, chef Michelle Hansen stuffs wild mushrooms into a tortilla for a savory take on a quesadilla. And Deborah Knight of Mosaic in Scottsdale makes an elegant vegetarian dish by combining quinoa, tofu, and Mexican cheese and herbs into a stuffing for squash blossoms.

In this profusion of new tastes and combinations, however, the old standards have not disappeared. The best of them continue to be favorites, and it is the rare Southwesterner or visitor to the region who can go too long without eating a taco or an enchilada. Spend a week in New Mexico and you're bound to be offered—and accept—a sopaipilla.

Here then are recipes from the cuisine of the new Southwest—totally original concepts along with some golden oldies that will always be served and never forgotten.

CHILES

Although Christopher Columbus set out on his voyage to find spices such as black pepper, what he encountered in the New World was not pepper, but chiles, which made their first appearance in Mexico around 7000 B.C.

Skip ahead six hundred-odd years and chiles have spread around the globe. Tucson chef Donna Nordin, of Terra Cotta, has called chiles both the foundation and the superstructure of Southwestern cooking. Not all Southwestern dishes contain chile, but you won't get far without knowing one variety from the other. Identical chiles can go by several different names and sometimes have a different name for both the fresh and dried forms. Chiles are frequently called chile peppers—thank Columbus for that. Another nomenclature oddity: Chile, with an "e," is the spice, while chili with an "i" is the dish made with meat, chile, and sometimes beans. Ground chile contains nothing but pure ground-up chile pods; chili powder contains other spices in addition to chile. Confused yet? (Since professional chefs prefer to control exactly the spices that go in their dishes, only pure ground chile is used in the recipes in this book.)

As a rule of thumb, the larger chile varieties are milder than the smaller ones. The heat is usually concentrated in the stem end as well as in the ribs and seeds. Capsaicin, an alkaloid, is the chemical compound that gives chiles their heat and, interestingly, is currently being studied as a stroke-preventive, is touted as helpful for allergies, and is used in pain-relieving creams. Other chemicals in chiles are potent antioxidants and may protect against such diseases as macular degeneration.

The relative spiciness of chiles is determined by their rating on the Scoville Scale, with zero for the mildest bell peppers and up to 400,000 for the hotter-than-hot habañeros. Individual chiles within a single variety can also vary in hotness due to growing conditions. As you can see from the Scoville scores noted in this list, a particularly hot Anaheim can be as hot as a mild jalapeño. It is always good to take a tiny taste before adding the full complement of chiles to any recipe.

Plant scientists at Texas A & M University have recently developed a less fiery habañero, which in its original form from Yucatán is incredibly hot. Called the TAM Mild Habañero, it is about as hot as the hotter range of the Anaheim. In the early 1980s, they developed a milder jalapeño, without which the craze for jalapeño poppers might never have flowered.

It is always wise to wear gloves when handling any chiles—their heat won't blister your hands, but you might forget and touch more sensitive skin on your face and eyes. Should you get a mouthful of something way too hot, neither water nor beer will help. Try milk or ice cream. The casein in the milk will attach to and wash away the capsaicin. If you do get a fleck of chile in your eye, quickly flush repeatedly with cool water.

Here is what you need to know about the varieties of chiles for the recipes included in this book, beginning with the mildest and moving through to the hottest.

ANAHEIMS *Scoville rating: 500–2,500*

This is the chile that appears on the long red strings (called "ristras") in many Southwestern markets. It is the most popular and most widely available chile. Anaheims are around six to seven inches long and green when fresh, turning shades of red when ripened. The green ones are canned and sold simply as "green chiles." The dried ones are sometimes labeled "California," which tend to be milder, or "New Mexico," which are hotter. When buying this type of chile ground, make sure you get pure chile. Chili (with an "i") powder has other spices included. Red chile powder is used in Sugar and Chile-Cured Venison Chops (page 163) and The Shed Posole (page 101). You can use green Anaheims in Chile con Queso (page 58), Gypsy Stew (page 99), Maria's New Mexican Green Chile Stew (page 100), Pink Adobe Steak Dunigan (page 144), and the Cotija Rabbit Rellenos (page 161).

POBLANOS *Scoville rating: 1,000–1,500*

Originally from the valley of Puebla in Mexico, these chiles are dark green, mild, and flavorful. They are from three to six inches in length and wider than the Anaheims. They are delicious in the Goat Cheese-Stuffed Poblano Chiles (page 179) and the Green Chile Macaroni (page 204).

ANCHOS *Scoville rating: 1,000-1,500*

Poblano chiles are called ancho chiles when dried. They become very dark, and the pod is a flat heart shape (the term "ancho" means "wide"). Use ancho chiles in Lamb Adobo (page 160) and Chorizo Potatoes (page 200).

PASILLAS *Scoville rating: 1,000–2,000*

Pasillas have a similar shape to the Anaheims, but are chocolate brown when fresh and ripe, and black when dried. If you find them, try them as a substitute for anchos in any recipes.

GUAJILLOS *Scoville rating: 1,500–4,000*

These chiles are a brownish orange when dried. They are easily confused with the Anaheim, but are a little narrower and have a fruitier, more complex flavor. They are frequently used in combination with Anaheims, however. When green they are called "mirasol" meaning "looking at the sun." Try guajillos in Black Guajillo Scallop Tostadas (page 67).

JALAPEÑOS *Scoville rating: 2,500–5,000*

These little green chiles vary from two to four inches long and are named for the town of Jalapa, Mexico, where they were first marketed. Jalapeños give a spicy kick to Steamed Dos Equis Clams (page 70) and Jalapeño–Blue Corn Muffins (page 47).

CHIPOTLES *Scoville rating: 2,500–5,000*

Available dried and canned in adobo sauce, chipotles are jalapeños that have been allowed to ripen to red, then dried and smoked over mesquite wood. Their heat-scale levels and Scoville scores are the same as for unsmoked jalapeños, but the spicy, dark adobo sauce they often come in enhances the heat, so use them sparingly. Chipotles offer a smoky note to White Cheddar–Chipotle Mashed Potatoes (page 199) and Spicy Grilled Chicken with Salad (page 132).

SERRANOS *Scoville rating: 5,000–15,000*

These chiles are bright green and look like small jalapeños. In fact, they can be used as a substitute for jalapeños although they are slightly hotter. You can use either serranos or jalapeños in Terra Cotta Salsa Fresca (page 211).

CHILES DE ÁRBOL *Scoville rating: 15,000–30,000*

These small, narrow chiles are green when fresh and red when dried—and they are fiery hot. Since they are so tiny, they can easily be minced very fine. They are an unexpected ingredient in the Peach, Chile, and Basil Tart (page 215).

CAYENNE *Scoville rating: 30,000–50,000*

These thin, very hot chiles are usually available dried and ground to a reddish powder. Just a sprinkle will usually do a great deal to pep up an otherwise bland dish. Cayenne gives a little zip to Stuffed Squash Blossoms (page 188) and Crispy Polenta with Gorgonzola Sauce (page 205).

HABAÑEROS *Scoville rating: 100,000–400,000*

A habañero looks like a thumb-sized yellow-orange bell pepper, but it is incredibly hot. Habañeros are used sparingly in Habañero Sea Scallops (page 61) and Monte Vista Tortilla Soup (page 93).

• • • • • • • • • • • • • • • • • • • •

Chefs frequently use more than one kind of chile to layer flavors in a single dish. Cream of Green Chile Soup (page 87) calls for both jalapeños and Anaheims. Stuffed Chicken Mole (page 127) combines ancho and guajillo chiles in its sauce. And Sweet Potato–Chicken Patties (page 25) are made with chipotles, while the Green Chile Hollandaise that tops them gets some zip from poblanos.

HOW TO ROAST AND PEEL CHILES AND BELL PEPPERS

The skin of fresh chiles and bell peppers is rather thick and waxy. In some recipes, this doesn't matter, but other recipes call for the skin to be removed, usually through roasting. Roasting chiles or bell peppers also adds a wonderful smoky flavor to them, essential to many Southwestern dishes. It is important to keep a close eye on the process, however. You want to stop the roasting at the point that the skin is charred but the interior flesh is still succulent. Here are several methods:

IN THE OVEN arrange whole chiles or halved bell peppers on a baking sheet (cut side down) and bake at 400 degrees F until they blister and the skins darken.

UNDER THE BROILER arrange whole chiles or halved bell peppers (cut side down) on a baking sheet and broil about 4 inches from the heat until the skins are blistered and charred. If roasting whole chiles, turn over with tongs once the top side is blistered.

ON THE GRILL OR GAS BURNER put whole chiles or whole peppers over a grill set to medium-high heat. Use tongs to turn until all sides are blackened. You can also spear individual chiles or peppers, or hold with tongs, directly above the flames of your gas stovetop, rotating until charred on all sides.

Once the chiles or peppers are blackened, transfer to a paper or plastic bag to steam for a few minutes. When cool enough to handle, the skins should easily peel off. An alternative to steaming is to immerse them in cold water before peeling. If you have difficulty removing the skins after roasting, hold under cold running water, then try again.

For some recipes, you will be cutting off the stems and pulling out the seeds before using the chile. If you want to modify the heat, also carefully slice or tear off the veins, as this is where the heat is concentrated. For rellenos and some other dishes, you will retain the stem and, instead, carefully make a slit in the side of the chile to clean out the seeds and veins.

breakfast and breads

baked artichoke omelette

THE PLEASANT STREET INN, PRESCOTT, ARIZONA

MAKES 6 SERVINGS

The invigorating climate in mile-high Prescott makes for hearty appetites. Generally, at bed-and-breakfasts like the pretty Pleasant Street Inn, located in a beautifully restored 1906 Victorian, guests expect to dine on luxurious dishes and to throw calorie caution to the winds. Proprietor Jeanne Watkins obliges with this delicious baked omelette. If you make this at home, however, you can cut down on the fat by using half as much cheese and substituting lowfat sour cream without an appreciable change in quality. A bowl of salsa on the side makes a nice addition.

½ cup defrosted and chopped frozen spinach

¾ cup medium-hot tomato salsa

1 can (8 ounces) artichoke hearts, drained and chopped

1 cup shredded Monterey Jack cheese

1 cup shredded medium cheddar cheese

6 eggs

8 ounces sour cream

PREHEAT THE OVEN to 350 degrees F. Drain chopped spinach in a sieve, pressing out excess moisture. Layer all ingredients in a 9-inch deep-dish pie plate, starting with salsa spread across bottom, followed by artichoke hearts and spinach. Combine Monterey Jack and cheddar cheeses and sprinkle over spinach. At this point, you can cover and refrigerate overnight if you wish. Bring back to room temperature to resume.

IN A MEDIUM BOWL, beat eggs, then stir in sour cream; pour egg mixture over the cheeses. Bake uncovered for 50 minutes or until omelette is completely set in the middle, like a custard, and top is lightly browned.

LET STAND for 5–10 minutes before serving.

eggs provençal

GHINI'S FRENCH CAFFE, TUCSON, ARIZONA

MAKES 1 SERVING

In an effort to support other local industries, chef Coralie Satta-Williams gets her hothouse tomatoes from Willcox, Arizona, where many small farms grow top-quality produce, and her bread from La Baguette Bakery in Tucson. "In my grandmother's kitchen, this dish was made in the oven, baked slowly with the garlic and thyme added at the end," she explains. "Of course that is not practical in a fast-paced restaurant atmosphere, so we gave it a little twist and prepare it in a sauté pan. Eat it with caution; it can be very addictive." At Ghini's they serve the eggs over easy, but you may scramble them if you prefer. Serve with a nice crusty French bread.

1 medium-size ripe tomato

Salt and pepper

3 tablespoons extra-virgin olive oil

1 tablespoon minced fresh garlic

2 large eggs

1 teaspoon chopped fresh thyme

THINLY SLICE AWAY ends from tomato, then cut tomato in half. Salt and pepper each half to taste.

WARM OLIVE OIL in sauté pan over medium heat. Add tomato halves, placing cut sides down. Cover and cook for 5 minutes or until tomato is softened and slightly caramelized. Flip tomatoes over and add minced garlic, cooking until garlic is lightly golden and aromatic. Add eggs to pan, cooking as desired, and sprinkle eggs and tomato with thyme. Continue cooking until eggs are done. Salt and pepper to taste and serve immediately.

MEXICAN CHEESES

For people who really enjoy cooking, one of the pleasures of trying new recipes is learning to use unfamiliar ingredients. For those experimenting with Southwestern cuisine, that means trying some of the delicious and unusual Mexican cheeses. To begin with, it is helpful to recognize that there are three different types of Mexican cheeses: mild fresh varieties, those best used for melting, and grating cheeses.

FRESH CHEESES

The fresh white Mexican cheeses do not melt well. This makes them excellent for use as a stuffing ingredient, because when heated, they become warm and soft but do not run. **Queso fresco,** also called **casero,** is similar to the more familiar farmer's cheese. It is the most traditional of the Mexican cheeses and is often used crumbled as a topping over beans. **Panela** is mild and milky tasting, similar to ricotta or a dry cottage cheese. **Queso blanco** is excellent for stuffing enchiladas, serving with vegetables, or straight snacking. It has a mild flavor and is also similar to farmer's cheese.

MELTING CHEESES

These cheeses are traditionally melted into hot dishes for dipping or pouring, as they do not separate into solids and oil when heated. They also make good, flavorful snacking cheeses. **Oaxaca** (wah-HAH-cah) is named after its Mexican state of origin and is a string cheese like mozzarella. Frequently sold as a woven ball, it is the best Mexican melting cheese. Similar to jack or Muenster cheese, **manchego** can be melted in a dish or paired with fruit as a snack. It has become a popular cheese in many Mediterranean or tapas restaurants. **Queso quesadilla** is just as it sounds—a soft, mild, processed cheese that makes excellent quesadillas (Mexico's version of America's beloved grilled-cheese sandwich). **Asadero** is a smooth, yellow cheese similar to provolone and has more tang than queso quesadilla.

DRY CHEESES

Cheeses in this category have a dry, crumbly texture and a strong flavor; they are good for grating. A bright white cheese that might be compared to Parmesan, **cotija** is sprinkled on top of refried beans or salads and can also be mixed into casseroles to enhance the flavor. It is named for the little Mexican village where it originated. Try it in the Cotija Rabbit Rellenos (page 161) or the Carnitas Napoleon (page 55). **Añejo enchilado** is a firm, pressed cheese that may look spicy, but the red powder on the outside is just mild paprika. It's most commonly used for enchiladas, tacos, and burritos.

tomato–basil–swiss cheese quiche

GARDEN COTTAGE BED AND BREAKFAST, CEDAR CITY, UTAH
MAKES 6 SERVINGS

Diana Simpkin, owner of the Garden Cottage Bed and Breakfast, devised this crustless quiche recipe after tasting something similar at another B&B. She says, "The delicious smells waft upstairs while cooking, and no one is ever late for breakfast on the mornings this is served! I sprinkle a little grated Swiss cheese on top, as well as fresh chopped chives from my garden." This charming inn is across the street from the site of the Utah Shakespearean Festival and is convenient to Zion National Park.

4 eggs
1 cup sour cream
1 cup cottage cheese
2 tablespoons flour
2 tablespoons cornmeal
1 teaspoon salt
1 teaspoon dried basil
⅛ teaspoon pepper
½ cup chopped green onions
1 cup chopped fresh tomatoes
2 cups shredded Swiss cheese
2 tablespoons chopped fresh chives

GREASE A GLASS PIE DISH or a 9 x 9-inch pan. Preheat the oven to 350 degrees F.

IN A MEDIUM BOWL, combine eggs, sour cream, cottage cheese, flour, cornmeal, salt, basil, and pepper until well mixed. Then carefully stir in green onions, tomatoes, and Swiss cheese, reserving a little of the cheese for garnish.

POUR EGG MIXTURE into the prepared pan. Bake for about 35–45 minutes or until quiche is set in the middle.

SPRINKLE WITH CHIVES and reserved cheese and serve hot.

baked egg soufflé

THE PLEASANT STREET INN, PRESCOTT, ARIZONA
MAKES 2 SERVINGS

The Pleasant Street Inn is just three blocks from the center of the Prescott Historic District and Courthouse Plaza. Prescott was Arizona's territorial capital, and much of the real Old West survives here, particularly in this neighborhood of Victorian homes. This dish calls for baking the eggs in ramekins; if you don't have any, you can use Pyrex sauce dishes or any small ovenproof ceramic containers.

4 eggs
⅓ cup light cream
½ cup shredded mild cheddar cheese, divided
Two green onions, thinly sliced, including some of the green
Cayenne pepper to taste

PREHEAT THE OVEN to 350 degrees F. Mix 2 eggs and all the cream together and set aside.

GENEROUSLY SPRINKLE half of the cheese in the bottoms of 2 nonstick ramekins that each hold at least ¾ cup when full. Top cheese with half of the sliced green onions. Crack 1 whole egg in the center of each ramekin, making sure not to break the yolk. Pour egg-cream mixture around the eggs. Top with more cheese and the rest of the onions. Sprinkle cayenne pepper on top for color and seasoning. At this point the eggs can be covered and stored in the refrigerator overnight. If held, bring back to room temperature before baking.

BAKE FOR 20 minutes or until eggs are puffy and almost firm. Serve immediately.

sweet potato–chicken patties with poached eggs and green chile hollandaise

BRYCE CANYON LODGE, BRYCE, UTAH

MAKES 4 SERVINGS

Bryce Canyon is home to more than one hundred species of birds, annually drawing flocks of birdwatchers who get up early—and are hungry when they finally make it in for breakfast. And this dish fills the bill. There is just the right amount of chile kick in the patties and in the hollandaise to give this dish a Southwestern flavor without overwhelming your mouth. This is also an excellent brunch dish for entertaining, as you can make the patties up to one day ahead. You'll have to make the hollandaise fresh, however, and if you have never made hollandaise sauce, don't try for the first time while you are greeting your guests! Read detailed instructions in a basic cookbook and practice, practice, practice.

SWEET POTATO–CHICKEN PATTIES
2 large sweet potatoes

3 boneless, skinless chicken breasts, about 6 ounces each

Salt and fresh-ground pepper to taste

1 large canned chipotle chile

3 scallions, thinly sliced

¼ cup coarsely chopped fresh cilantro

1 tablespoon honey

2 tablespoons olive oil

GREEN CHILE HOLLANDAISE
3 large egg yolks, lightly beaten

1 tablespoon fresh lemon juice

1 stick (½ cup) unsalted butter, melted

1 large poblano chile, roasted, peeled, seeds removed, and finely chopped (see page 14)

Pinch of ground cayenne pepper

¼ teaspoon salt

POACHED EGGS
3 cups water
1 tablespoon white wine vinegar
4 eggs

FOR THE PATTIES, peel potatoes and cut into ½-inch cubes. In a small saucepan, cover the cubed potatoes with cold water and bring to a boil over high heat. Reduce the heat and simmer just until tender, about 7–9 minutes. Drain.

MEANWHILE, HEAT A MEDIUM SAUCEPAN with about 4 inches of water until just simmering. Season chicken breasts with salt and pepper and place in the simmering water; add more water to just cover if necessary. Poach chicken until just cooked through, about 8–10 minutes. Remove from water, drain, and when cool enough to handle, cut each breast into ½-inch cubes.
Finely chop the chipotle chile until it has a puree consistency. You should have about 1 tablespoon.

COMBINE POTATOES, chicken, chipotle puree, scallions, cilantro, and honey in a large bowl and mix gently, then season with salt and pepper to taste. Form into 4 patties, each about 1 inch thick and 3 inches across. At this point you can refrigerate the patties for up to 24 hours. Remove them from the refrigerator 30 minutes before cooking to bring to room temperature.

HEAT OLIVE OIL on high in large skillet until just starting to smoke, then turn down heat to low. Preheat the oven to 200 degrees F. Cook patties until lightly browned and crisp, about 3 minutes on each side. Remove to plate and keep warm in oven.

FOR THE GREEN CHILE HOLLANDAISE, combine egg yolks and lemon juice in top of a double boiler, or in a medium stainless steel bowl that you can set over a pan of water. Whisk eggs until frothy. Place over simmering water (do not let the bottom actually touch the water) and continue whisking the yolks until pale yellow and fluffy, 2–4 minutes, making sure they don't get too hot. Gradually add the melted butter 1 tablespoon at a time, whisking until incorporated.

REMOVE EGGS FROM HEAT and fold in poblano chile, cayenne pepper, and ¼ teaspoon salt or to taste. If the sauce gets too hot it may separate; if so, put it into a blender to reincorporate. Keep the sauce warm over hot water or in a warm oven while you poach the eggs.

FOR THE POACHED EGGS, heat water and vinegar in a deep skillet until simmering. Break an egg into a teacup and then gently slip the egg into the water. Repeat with remaining eggs. Poach 4–5 minutes, or until the whites have set and the yolks are still a bit jiggly.

TO SERVE, place the patties on 4 individual plates and set an egg on top of each. Drizzle with Green Chile Hollandaise and serve immediately, with extra hollandaise available on the side.

banana french toast with pecan streusel and amaretto sauce

CASA SEDONA BED AND BREAKFAST INN, SEDONA, ARIZONA

MAKES 6 SERVINGS

Casa Sedona Bed and Breakfast Inn is both spectacular and cozy. It was designed by a protégé of Frank Lloyd Wright to maximize the surrounding views of the dramatic red rock cliffs. The area offers fishing, hiking trails, interesting shopping, and compelling art galleries. Guests at Casa Sedona get a good sendoff on their busy days with breakfasts such as this rich and satisfying French toast. The recipe calls for "Texas bread," referring to large, soft white loaves, sold unsliced. Italian bread with a soft crust can substitute. The Amaretto Sauce is wonderful, but optional. This recipe is organized so that you start it the night before, making morning preparation quick.

FRENCH TOAST
4 ripe bananas, mashed (about 2 cups)
1 can evaporated milk (12 ounces)
3 eggs, beaten
½ cup sugar
1 tablespoon vanilla extract
¼ teaspoon almond extract
1 teaspoon cinnamon
7 thick slices Texas bread, cut into ¾-inch cubes

STREUSEL
1 teaspoon cinnamon
¼ cup brown sugar
2 tablespoons flour
1 tablespoon melted butter
½ cup chopped pecans

AMARETTO SAUCE
1 cup butter (2 sticks)
2 cups powdered sugar
½ cup Amaretto or other almond-flavored liqueur
2 egg yolks

3 ripe bananas, sliced 3/8-inch thick
Maple syrup (optional)

FOR THE FRENCH TOAST, stir together bananas, milk, eggs, sugar, vanilla extract, almond extract, and cinnamon in a large bowl. Place bread cubes in a lightly greased 9 x 13-inch pan. Pour egg mixture evenly over bread.

FOR THE STREUSEL, combine in a small bowl all ingredients. Sprinkle over bread and egg mixture. Cover tightly and refrigerate overnight.

REMOVE FRENCH TOAST from refrigerator 30 minutes before cooking; preheat the oven to 350 degrees F. Bake for about 40–45 minutes or until streusel is lightly browned. Let stand 10 minutes before cutting into 6 large squares.

FOR THE AMARETTO SAUCE, melt butter and sugar together in a small saucepan over low heat. Add Amaretto and egg yolks; continue cooking for 2 more minutes, stirring regularly.

SERVE FRENCH TOAST SQUARES with sliced bananas and drizzled Amaretto Sauce or maple syrup.

decadent french toast

BIG YELLOW INN BED AND BREAKFAST, CEDAR CITY, UTAH

MAKES 8 SERVINGS

The Big Yellow Inn is indeed large and yellow. Guests staying at the Georgian Revival inn get pampered with luscious breakfasts, including this baked French toast. The inn typically serves it with berries and sour cream on top; poached apple slices or other fruits are also delicious. Take your cream cheese out of the refrigerator in time for it to soften so you can spread it easily on the bread. For best results, use good quality bakery-style bread rather than the spongy kind.

16 slices firm bread
4 ounces cream cheese, softened
Cinnamon and granulated sugar to taste
1 cup brown sugar
½ cup butter (1 stick)
¾ cup maple syrup
6 large eggs
1¾ cup milk
1 teaspoon vanilla extract
2 cups mixed berries (raspberries, strawberries, blueberries, and/or blackberries)
Sour cream for garnish

SPREAD 8 SLICES of bread with cream cheese and sprinkle with cinnamon and sugar. Top each with another slice of bread. Cut "sandwiches" in half diagonally.

IN A MEDIUM SAUCEPAN, combine brown sugar, butter, and maple syrup. Cook over low heat 5 minutes until dissolved. Transfer mixture to an 11 x 17-inch baking pan and spread to cover the bottom. Add sandwich halves to pan. In separate bowl, blend together eggs, milk, and vanilla extract. Pour over bread. Cover and let sit 45 minutes or overnight in fridge. If refrigerated, bring to room temperature while you preheat the oven to 350 degrees F.

UNCOVER AND BAKE for 30–40 minutes, until the top layer has browned and the bottom sugar-syrup mixture has caramelized. Remove pieces to plates or platter, flipping so caramel side is up. Top each serving with berries and a dollop of sour cream.

sausage en croûte

SEVEN WIVES INN BED AND BREAKFAST, ST. GEORGE, UTAH

MAKES 6–8 SERVINGS

St. George is conveniently located to access some of the Southwest's most scenic treasures: Zion and Bryce Canyons, Lake Powell, and the north rim of the Grand Canyon. Guests at the Seven Wives Inn not only get a good sleep and a nourishing breakfast, but also afternoon tea and, for a real indulgence, a massage after a day of hiking or golfing. This recipe is a Seven Wives original. The directions let you prepare everything partially the night before so you can finish it quickly in the morning.

SAUSAGE FILLING
3–4 green onions, including some tops, chopped
5–6 medium button mushrooms, sliced
1 tablespoon butter
1 pound bulk (country-style) pork sausage
3 ounces Monterey Jack cheese, grated

CRUST
½ cup (1 stick) butter
¾ cup lowfat cottage cheese
1 cup flour

FOR THE SAUSAGE FILLING, sauté onions and mushrooms in a little butter until onion is translucent; remove from heat and set aside. In same pan, brown sausage, breaking until crumbly, until pink has disappeared, about 8–10 minutes; set aside. Grate cheese. Refrigerate each in 3 separate containers until morning.

FOR THE CRUST, in a food processor mix butter and cottage cheese until mostly blended, but leaving some pea-size butter pieces. Add flour and pulse the machine on and off until just blended. If not using a food processor, cream cottage cheese by whirling in a blender or pressing through a sieve. Cut butter into flour with a pastry cutter as if you were making a pie crust. Add cottage cheese and stir lightly until blended. Turn out mixture onto plastic wrap, form into a ball, and refrigerate overnight or for at least 2 hours.

IN THE MORNING, preheat the oven to 350 degrees F. Remove dough from refrigerator and immediately roll out on a floured board to about 10 inches by 14 inches. Fold into fourths and, using a large spatula, transfer to a lightly greased baking sheet large enough to hold it. Unfold pastry and spread sausage down the center third going lengthwise, then add mushroom-onion mixture, and top all with grated cheese. Starting 4 inches from the top, slice the exposed crust on each side into 4 strips, each about 1½ inches wide. You should also have 4 inches left at the bottom. Fold strips up, first one side and then the other, lapping over filling to form a sort of lattice across the top. Pinch and fold under the ends to make a tidy package. Bake for 30 minutes or until crust is golden brown. Slice crosswise into 6–8 serving pieces.

southwestern biscuits
with sausage and crayfish gravy

REMINGTON'S, SCOTTSDALE PLAZA RESORT, SCOTTSDALE, ARIZONA
MAKES 4 SERVINGS

Many early Western pioneers and cowboys subsisted on biscuits and gravy. Biscuits could be baked in a Dutch oven set over coals from an open fire. Cowhands expected a pan of biscuits when they returned to the chuck wagon after a long day riding fence or looking after cattle. This dish, a lavish version of the old favorite, was developed by Richard Sederholt, the award-winning chef at Remington's at the Scottsdale Plaza Resort. If you can't find crayfish tail meat, you can substitute shrimp. Most frozen crayfish comes parboiled, but if you are starting with fresh, boil for five minutes, then pick from the shells. As for the biscuits, you can make your own favorite recipe, get them from a bakery, or choose partially prepared biscuits available in the refrigerated case at the grocery store. Chef Sederholt uses his own special seasoning mixture (recipe follows) for the gravy.

SAUSAGE AND CRAYFISH GRAVY
2 tablespoons butter
¼ cup finely chopped onion
1 pound spicy chicken sausage, meat removed from casing
1 tablespoon flour
1 cup chicken stock
1 cup heavy cream
½ pound crayfish tail meat (see recipe introduction)
1 tablespoon chopped fresh parsley
1 teaspoon Chef Rick's Southwestern Seasoning (recipe follows)
Cayenne pepper to taste
Salt and black pepper to taste

4 large baking-powder biscuits, warmed

GARNISH
2 tablespoons chopped fresh parsley
1 red bell pepper, cored, seeds removed, and cut into ¼-inch strips

FOR THE GRAVY, in a heavy medium-size saucepan, melt butter over medium heat. Add the onions and sauté for 2 minutes until slightly transparent, then add chicken sausage and sauté until it crumbles and is cooked through, approximately 3–4 minutes.

SPRINKLE FLOUR over the sausage mixture and stir in. Turn heat to low and cook for 5 more minutes to cook the flour.

ADD CHICKEN STOCK to the saucepan, a little at a time, incorporating with a wire wisk. Turn heat back up to medium, stirring often until mixture comes to a boil and thickens. After the mixture thickens, add cream. Continue heating until it is a medium-consistency gravy. If it gets too thick, add 1 teaspoon of chicken stock or milk at a time to thin; if it's too thin, continue cooking over medium heat until it reduces, but be careful not to burn the gravy.

WHEN GRAVY IS READY, add crayfish and chopped fresh parsley; heat through, about 2–3 minutes. Season with Chef Rick's Southwestern Seasoning. Taste, then add cayenne pepper, salt, and black pepper if desired.

WARM BISCUITS in a 250-degree F oven, or follow directions on the package. Split in half and place on plates; top with gravy and garnish each half with a sprinkle of chopped parsley and 3 red pepper strips.

CHEF RICK'S SOUTHWESTERN SEASONING

MIX 3 PARTS ground red chile with 1 part each granulated garlic, ground cumin seed, gumbo filé powder, Mexican oregano, ground black pepper, cayenne pepper, cinnamon, ground allspice, paprika, onion powder, dried basil, kosher salt, ground nutmeg, and dried thyme. Adjust spicy heat by increasing the cayenne pepper. You can use this to season any dish that needs a little zip. Try it as a pork rub or sprinkle in a chile sauce.

seven wives inn granola

SEVEN WIVES INN BED AND BREAKFAST, ST. GEORGE, UTAH
MAKES ABOUT 18 SERVINGS (1 CUP EACH)

Comprised of two neighboring homes as well as a cottage, Seven Wives Inn is named in honor of one of the ancestors of the current innkeeper, Brent Calder. When polygamy was outlawed in 1882, Calder's Mormon great-great grandfather, who indeed had seven wives, used to hide out from the law in the larger of the two homes. Donna Curtis, the original founder of the inn, created this granola recipe for guests to dip into on busy mornings.

8 cups old-fashioned oats
1½ cups brown sugar
½ cup mild vegetable oil
½ cup smooth peanut butter
½ cup water
2 cups cashew halves
2 cups sliced almonds
2 cups sunflower seeds
2 cups coconut flakes

COMBINE FIRST 5 INGREDIENTS in a medium saucepan and cook over medium-low heat, stirring well, until all peanut butter is dissolved.

COMBINE NUTS, seeds, and coconut in a large bowl. Add oat mixture and combine well.

HEAT OVEN to 150 degrees F. Spread out granola evenly on a nonstick, greased cookie sheet. Bake for 1 hour. Crack the oven door and turn off the oven. Let sit in the oven with the door cracked overnight or until granola dries. Break apart and store in an airtight container for up to 3 weeks. Refrigerate for longer storage.

prickly pear–date sticky buns

FURNACE CREEK INN, DEATH VALLEY NATIONAL PARK, CALIFORNIA

MAKES 8 BUNS

Dates and prickly pear fruit—both products of the desert—are combined here by chef Michelle Hansen. Chef Mic, as she is called, presides over the inn's kitchen during the winters at Death Valley National Park. The park comprises 3.3 million acres and is one of the hottest and driest places in the world. But despite this sometimes harsh climate, Death Valley is home to more than 970 species of plants.

DOUGH
2 cups sifted all-purpose flour
1 tablespoon baking powder
1 teaspoon salt
¼ teaspoon baking soda
¼ cup vegetable oil
¾ cup buttermilk

FILLING
½ cup prickly pear jelly (see Resources)
¼ cup (½ stick) butter, softened
½ cup chopped pecans
¼ cup chopped dates
¼ cup sugar
½ teaspoon cinnamon

ICING
1 tablespoon prickly pear jelly
1 tablespoon cream cheese, softened
½ teaspoon powdered sugar
1 tablespoon cream
¼ teaspoon cinnamon

COMBINE FLOUR, baking powder, salt, and baking soda in a bowl. Mix well, then gradually stir in oil. Add buttermilk, stirring just until blended. Knead dough on a lightly floured surface until smooth. Cover with a damp towel and let rest for 30 minutes.

WHILE THE DOUGH IS RESTING, combine all filling ingredients in a bowl and stir until well blended.

PREHEAT THE OVEN to 400 degrees F. Lightly grease pie tin or 8- or 9-inch cake pan and set aside.

ROLL OUT DOUGH on floured surface to approximately 8 x 15 inches. Spread filling evenly over the dough. Starting at a short end, roll up the dough to the other end, pinwheel style. Pinch the seam to seal. Cut the roll into 8 slices 1-inch thick. Arrange slices cut side up in the prepared baking pan.

BAKE UNTIL LIGHTLY BROWNED, about 20 minutes.

FOR THE ICING, while rolls are baking, combine all ingredients in a small bowl using a wire whisk, which helps break up and combine the jelly.

REMOVE ROLLS FROM OVEN, invert onto a dish, and drizzle with icing. These are best eaten the day they are made.

orange–cranberry english scones

THE GARDEN COTTAGE BED AND BREAKFAST, CEDAR CITY, UTAH

MAKES 8 SCONES

Lucky guests at the Garden Cottage Bed and Breakfast, a historic home with all the charm and characteristics of a quaint English cottage, might get these wonderful scones for breakfast. Owner Diana Simpkin got the recipe from her youngest daughter, Hailey, who has enjoyed cooking since she was a little girl. Diana usually serves these scones with fresh butter and a variety of toppings to choose from: jams, Nutella, jellies, homemade raspberry butter, and lemon curd.

3 cups flour
6 tablespoons sugar
1 tablespoon baking powder
Pinch of salt
Zest of 1 orange
½ cup (1 stick) butter
⅔ cup buttermilk
1 tablespoon orange juice concentrate
Juice of 1 orange
1 cup dried cranberries
1 egg yolk

PREHEAT THE OVEN to 425 degrees F. Mix together flour, sugar, baking powder, salt, and zest in a medium-size bowl. Slice butter into pieces; using a pastry blender, cut butter into flour mixture until crumbly.

POUR IN THE BUTTERMILK and stir with a fork until the mixture holds together. Add juices and cranberries and continue mixing.

GATHER THE DOUGH into a ball and gently knead a few times on a lightly floured surface. Pat out dough into an 8-inch-diameter circle and cut into 8 equal wedges. Place wedges on a greased and floured baking sheet. Brush the tops with egg yolk. Bake for 20–25 minutes. Serve warm with your choice of toppings.

apple fritters

WAUNITA HOT SPRINGS RANCH, GUNNISON, COLORADO

MAKES ABOUT 30 FRITTERS

Waunita Hot Springs Ranch is a family oriented dude ranch, located high in the Colorado Rockies just ten miles west of the Continental Divide. Three generations of the Pringle family make it their home and their livelihood. These fritters are a guest favorite during the ranch's popular outdoor cookouts. Be careful the oil doesn't get too hot, however, or the fritters will brown before the insides are cooked through. Choose apples that cook well and retain their flavor, such as Empire, Jonathan, or Braeburn.

2 cups grated apples (about 5 medium-size apples)
2 tablespoons milk
2 eggs, beaten
1 tablespoon melted butter or margarine
1 cup flour
3 tablespoons sugar
1 teaspoon baking powder
½ teaspoon salt
¼ teaspoon cinnamon
Dash of ground nutmeg
3 cups vegetable oil
1 cup powered sugar

MIX ALL INGREDIENTS together, except oil and powdered sugar, to make a soft batter. You can make the batter up to a couple of hours ahead and refrigerate. If you make the batter ahead of time, you may need to add a little flour to thicken it before cooking, as the apples release juice while they sit.

HEAT OIL in a deep heavy saucepan to 350–360 degrees F. Drop batter by rounded teaspoonfuls into the hot oil, about 6 at a time. Cook until golden brown, 30–60 seconds on a side, turning once. Remove with a slotted spoon and set on paper towels to drain. Keep warm in an oven set to 250 degrees F. Adjust heat to maintain the temperature of the oil. Repeat until all the batter is gone.

PUT POWERED SUGAR into a large zip-lock bag or a medium-size paper bag. Add cooked fritters, in 2 or 3 batches, seal bag, and shake to cover fritters in sugar. Serve immediately.

nutball coffee cake

THE GARDEN COTTAGE BED AND BREAKFAST, CEDAR CITY, UTAH

MAKES AN 8-INCH ROUND CAKE

Diana Simpkin, proprietor of the romantic Garden Cottage B&B, inherited this coffee cake recipe from her dear friend Karlene Paxman, who opened the first bed-and-breakfast in Cedar City. The balls of dough rise together but pull apart easily for serving once the cake is baked. Diana drizzles cream cheese icing over the cake and serves it warm on a round platter in the center of the table. She says, "There are always oohs and aahs when I place it on the table." Guests often ask for the recipe. Use a self-rising baking mix such as Bisquick.

¼ cup (½ stick) butter

¾ cup brown sugar

4 teaspoons cinnamon, divided

1 cup finely chopped pecans

2 cups baking mix

5 tablespoons sugar

1 teaspoon ground nutmeg

1 egg, beaten

⅓ cup milk

ICING

1 cup powdered sugar

2 tablespoons cream cheese, softened

1–3 tablespoons milk

PREHEAT THE OVEN to 375 degrees F. Grease a deep 8-inch pie pan. Melt butter in a small bowl and set aside. Combine brown sugar and 3 teaspoons cinnamon in a shallow bowl and set aside. Put chopped pecans in a shallow bowl and set aside.

IN A MEDIUM BOWL, blend baking mix, sugar, remaining teaspoon of cinnamon, and nutmeg. In a cup, beat egg, add milk, and combine. Add to the dry mixture and beat to combine thoroughly. The dough will be very soft. Using a heaping teaspoonful at a time, dip the dough first in the melted butter, then in brown sugar–cinnamon, and finally in nuts. Place balls closely together in the greased pie pan. Bake about 20–25 minutes until nicely browned on top. Remove from oven. Turn out the coffee cake onto a plate, then put a second plate on the bottom of the coffee cake and flip so the top rounded side is up.

FOR THE ICING, in a medium bowl, combine the powered sugar and cream cheese and 1 tablespoon of milk to make a thin frosting; add another 1 or 2 tablespoons of milk if the icing seems too thick. Drizzle the frosting in an artistic pattern over the warm coffee cake.

USE A FORK to pull off pieces of cake.

PECANS

Anyone traveling along major highways in the southern part of the Southwest region has noticed the pecan orchards—orderly rows of trees, lush green in summer, leafless in winter. From far west Texas through the southern parts of New Mexico and Arizona and on into California, pecans are a major commercial crop. For example, the Green Valley area south of Tucson, Arizona, alone produces 8 million pounds of pecans a year from 6,000 acres. In fact, half of the top-ten pecan-producing counties are in the Southwest, and Texas considers the crop so important it has adopted the pecan as its state tree.

Pecans (species name *Carya illinoensis*) ripen from mid-September to December and are harvested when they fall to the ground. The familiar shell is covered with a husk that is removed once the nut is thoroughly dry. Although most of us get our pecans from a grocery store, these nuts can be raised by the home gardener who is willing to make sure the trees get enough water and fertilizer to produce plump and tasty kernels. Most plant experts advise that pecan trees don't do well above 3,700 feet in elevation because of the danger of frost damage.

Pecans are native to North America and are a member of the walnut family. Native varieties produce nuts that are smaller and drier than what we're used to, but pecans have been improved over the years by cultivators. Many of the newer varieties are named after Native Americans, for whom pecans were a major food source. Popular types include Apache, Choctaw, Cheyenne, Mohawk, Sioux, and Wichita.

The earliest planting of an improved varietal was near Mesilla, New Mexico, in 1915. Other plantings in New Mexico and Arizona followed in the 1920s and 1930s, but pecans didn't become an economically important crop until the 1960s, because they were too expensive relative to the wages people earned.

Pecans remain fresh longer if they are stored in the shell, so buy them in shells if you don't intend to use them right away. Once they are shelled they should be stored in air-tight containers in the refrigerator and can be kept for up to nine months.

The high fat content in pecans make them high in calories, but that oil is rich in oleic acid, the healthful fatty acid found in olive oil. Pecans are also rich in vitamins, minerals, antioxidants, and fiber. They add richness and a satisfying crunch to foods such as Banana French Toast with Pecan Streusel and Amaretto Sauce (page 27), Nutball Coffee Cake (page 39), Caramel Pecan Cheesecake (page 220), and Texas Millionaire Pie (page 217).

sopaipillas

RANCHO DE CHIMAYO, CHIMAYO, NEW MEXICO
MAKES 12 SOPAIPILLAS

If you eat at the popular Rancho de Chimayo, you *will* get sopaipillas—they are served with everything! When the restaurant is busy in the height of summer, the kitchen often makes nearly 4,000 sopaipillas every day. This recipe calls for a slightly sweet sopaipilla, perfect for eating drizzled with honey. Rancho de Chimayo chefs suggest using rice bran oil if you can find it, because it works especially well when frying at high temperatures. A cooking thermometer that registers up to at least 410 degrees F is strongly suggested for this recipe, which requires that great care be used around the hot cooking oil.

2 cups flour
1 teaspoon salt
1 teaspoon baking powder
1½ teaspoons sugar, optional
1½ teaspoons canola or corn oil
½ cup lukewarm water
¼ cup evaporated milk, at room temperature
4 cups oil, preferably rice bran oil, but canola and corn oils work too
Honey, as an accompaniment

SIFT TOGETHER FLOUR, salt, baking powder, and sugar into a large mixing bowl. Pour oil into the dry ingredients and mix with your fingertips to combine. Add water and milk, working the liquids into the dough until a sticky ball forms.

LIGHTLY DUST a counter or pastry board with flour and knead the dough vigorously for 1 minute. The mixture should be "earlobe" soft and no longer sticky. Let the dough rest, covered with a damp cloth, for 15 minutes. Divide the dough into 3 balls, covering each with the damp cloth, and let them rest again for another 15–30 minutes. If not using immediately, the dough can be refrigerated up to 4 hours.

DUST A COUNTER or pastry board lightly with flour and roll out each ball of dough into a circle or oval approximately ¼ inch thick. Rim off any ragged edges and discard them. To avoid toughening the dough, it should be rolled out only once. With a sharp knife, cut each circle of dough into 4 equal wedges. Cover the wedges with the damp cloth. Don't stack the wedges, because they are likely to stick together.

LAYER SEVERAL THICKNESSES of paper towels near the stove. In a wok or a high-sided, heavy skillet, heat the rice bran oil over high heat to 400 degrees F. Give the oil your full attention so that, while it is heating, the temperature does not exceed 400 degrees F. If the oil smokes before reaching the proper temperature, it cannot be used for this recipe because there is a danger of it catching fire. To avoid this, make sure you are using fresh, high-quality oil.

EXERCISING CARE to avoid a possible burn, gently drop a wedge of dough into the hot oil. After sinking in the oil briefly, it should begin to balloon and rise back to the surface. Cautiously spoon some of the oil over the sopaipilla after it begins to float. When the top surface has fully puffed—just a matter of seconds—turn the sopaipilla over with tongs, again being extremely cautious. Cook it until it is just a light golden color, remove it with tongs, and drain it on the paper towels. If a sopaipilla darkens before it is fully puffed, decrease the temperature by a few degrees before frying the remaining dough.

MAKE 2–3 SOPAIPILLAS at a time, adjusting the heat as necessary to keep the oil's temperature consistent. Arrange the fried breads in a napkin-lined basket and serve immediately with honey.

CORN

Corn is the staff of life for the Southwest. It developed originally somewhere in the Mexico–Guatemala border region and then spread south into South America and north through northern Mexico to the southwestern United States, before traveling throughout the Americas. It was not known in Europe, Asia, or Africa until Columbus introduced it.

A type of grass, corn grows only where there are farmers to care for and cultivate it. Some annuals reseed themselves, but generally corn must be planted by a human being at exactly the perfect time to have the right temperature and moisture conditions for growth. And, unlike most of our food plants, nothing similar to corn grows in the wild. Even its closest relative, teosinte, does not produce cobs and kernels.

That leaves us with a mystery. If there was no wild form of corn for the ancient populations to develop and domesticate, how did it come into being as a food plant? Many scientists have devoted their entire professional lives to this conundrum.

What we do know is that early corn was much different from what we have today; the cobs and kernels, for instance, were very small. Thousands of years of breeding by early farmers led to the larger ears that we have today, making corn the earliest genetically engineered crop.

Native cooks developed early methods of making corn, with its tough outer shell, palatable and digestible. They ground the kernels between two rocks to make a meal that could then be combined with water to make mush. Later they learned to remove the hard hulls by soaking the kernels in water with ashes. The result they called *nixtamal*. We call it posole or hominy. Nixtamal remains an important ingredient in soup, such as The Shed Posole (page 101), and is also ground into a dough called *masa*, which is the basis for corn tortillas. Corn tortillas are used in Carnitas Napoleon (page 55), Monte Vista Tortilla Soup (page 93), Sonoran Tortilla Soup (page 95), Canyon Ranch Grilled Chicken Enchiladas (page 128), Tostadas Compuestas (page 155), and the Pan-Seared Salmon Tostada (page 168).

One of southern Arizona's great delicacies is the green corn tamale. The corn from which this dish is made isn't actually green. In fact, it's just field corn that is picked "green" or unripened. Before the availability of the many types of sweet corn with their tender hulls, white varieties of field or flour corn were picked green before the exterior of the kernels had coarsened. The green corn kernels are ground, then combined with cheese and green chile strips, wrapped in corn husks, and steamed. A lowfat version of this dish can be enjoyed with the recipe for Canyon Ranch Tamales (page 184).

Blue corn is a flour-corn variety, traditionally grown by Hopi and various Pueblo Indian tribes, and has a subtle, earthy, sweet flavor. The color is really a deep purple and is only as deep as the kernel's skin. Blue corn was used traditionally in dumplings, tortillas, and gravies, but today many grocery stores carry blue corn tortillas and blue corn chips. The recipes for Jalapeño–Blue Corn Muffins (page 47) and Blue-Corn-Crusted Rainbow Trout (page 170) reflect modern uses for blue corn.

The continuing popularity of corn on Southwest menus and dinner tables is reflected in other ways—both traditional and creative—throughout this book. Corn in its various forms appears in Garlic-Sautéed Lobster Medallions with Corn Blinis (page 59), Palace Corn Chowder (page 90), El Tovar Fire-Roasted Corn Salsa (page 209), Crayfish–Corn Risotto (page 173), Crispy Polenta with Gorgonzola Sauce (page 205), Roasted Corn and Sage Mashed Potatoes (page 203), Southwestern Succotash (page 207), Corn Risotto (page 201), and even a dessert, the Cornmeal–Lime Cookie (page 224).

mustard seed and onion flatbread

LON'S AT THE HERMOSA, PHOENIX, ARIZONA

MAKES 65–70 CRACKERS, OR ENOUGH FLATBREAD TO COVER 2 LARGE BAKING SHEETS

The term "flatbread" comes from the Norwegian "flatbrod." They are crisp, like what we call a cracker. Most of us are used to getting crackers out of a box, but they are actually easy to make. Try the basic formula here, and then improvise freely. Replace the mustard seed with pumpkin seeds, piñon nuts (pine nuts), or sesame seeds. Try adding minced fresh herbs like fennel tops or marjoram when adding the onion. Using all white flour creates a lighter product. The amount of water will depend on how dry the flour is—you'll use less in humid areas, more in drier climates. You may also find that your crackers develop more flavor the second or third day after baking as the flavorings expand into the crackers. If you do use sesame seeds, try substituting sesame oil for some of the butter. Flatbreads are traditionally served with cheese, and as an accompaniment to soups and salads.

2 tablespoons mustard seed
1½ cups all-purpose flour
½ cup whole wheat flour
1 teaspoon salt
1 teaspoon pepper
½ cup unsalted butter
1 cup minced white onion
10–12 tablespoons water
Kosher salt for cooking

PREHEAT THE OVEN to 375 degrees F. Process mustard seeds into a fine meal using a food mill, spice mill, or coffee grinder, and then combine with the all-purpose flour, whole wheat flour, salt, and pepper. Cut the butter into the flour mixture until it resembles coarse meal. Mix in the onion and enough water to form a firm ball.

DIVIDE THE DOUGH into 2 parts and roll half out to about ⅛-inch thickness. Prick the dough by poking holes in it with the tines of a fork, then cut into 2-inch squares or other desired shapes. You can also leave the dough in one large sheet. Transfer to an ungreased baking sheet or pan. Repeat with the other half of the dough.

BAKE FOR 15–20 MINUTES, giving the pan a 180-degree turn twice through the cooking process to help cook evenly. Check how the dough is browning each time you turn the pan, as even a small deviation in the oven temperature can cause it to over-brown. Remove when the flatbread is evenly and lightly browned. Cool before serving or before storing in a tightly covered container for up to 4 days. These crackers are best when eaten fresh.

jalapeño–blue corn muffins

TALL TIMBER RESORT, DURANGO, COLORADO
MAKES 12 REGULAR-SIZE MUFFINS, OR 36 "MINI" MUFFINS

No roads, no stress, no telephones, no deadlines—when you are at Tall Timber Resort, 180 private acres in the middle of the San Juan National Forest, you are truly away from it all. What you aren't away from is delicious food—which is good, because all that refreshing mountain air is an appetite stimulant. There are fresh-baked goods served every day. Blue corn has been grown by Native Americans for centuries (see pages 44–45 for a longer discussion). Chef/owner Judy Beggrow uses cornmeal that she says is "a beautiful shade of blue" to make these muffins. These make a good accompaniment to any kind of soup or stew.

DRY INGREDIENTS
½ cup blue cornmeal (see Resources)
1½ cups plus 2 tablespoons cake flour
7 tablespoons sugar
2 teaspoons baking powder
¼ teaspoon salt

WET INGREDIENTS
¾ cup whole milk
½ cup unsalted butter, melted
2 large eggs, beaten
¾ cup whole corn kernels, drained (½ of a 15-ounce can)
¼ cup finely diced red bell peppers
¼ cup finely diced green bell peppers
2 tablespoons finely chopped jalapeño chiles

PREHEAT THE OVEN to 400 degrees F. Grease muffin tins.

COMBINE DRY INGREDIENTS in a large bowl and stir well. Combine wet ingredients in medium bowl and blend. Pour wet ingredients over dry ingredients and stir just until moistened. Do not over mix. Cover with plastic wrap and refrigerate at least 6 hours. Divide batter into 12 muffin cups. Bake at 400 degrees F for 12–15 minutes or until a toothpick inserted in a muffin center comes out clean. Unmold immediately to serve warm, or reheat before serving in a 250-degree F oven for 10 minutes.

appetizers

anasazi bean-dip boats

TALL TIMBER RESORT, DURANGO, COLORADO
MAKES 10 SERVINGS

Luxurious Tall Timber Resort is truly a get-away-from-it-all spot outside of Durango. The nearest road is six miles away, so arrival is only by the Durango-Silverton narrow-gauge railroad or helicopter. Chef Judy Beggrow devised this appetizer—a much glorified version of chips and bean dip—using Anasazi beans grown eighty miles west of Durango in the small farming community of Dove Creek. (If Anasazi beans are not available, you can substitute pintos.) The ancho chiles she uses in the Red Chile Pesto that complements the beans are also grown nearby. These charming little bean "boats" are finished with a refreshing Lime Crème Fraîche. Although served as an appetizer at Tall Timber, this can also serve as a side dish for a meal of tamales, rellenos, or enchiladas. Chicken base comes in a jar and is used like bouillon, but has less salt and more real flavor. You can substitute bouillon. Several hours before you plan to assemble the appetizer, soak the corn husks in warm water to make them pliable.

ANASAZI BEAN FILLING
1 pound Anasazi beans (see Resources)
2½ tablespoons chicken base
½ large onion, diced
1 cup loosely packed chopped fresh cilantro leaves
⅓ cup diced green bell pepper
⅓ cup diced red bell pepper
⅓ cup diced yellow bell pepper
1 can (4 ounces) diced green chiles, drained
¼ teaspoon Tabasco
1 teaspoon cayenne pepper
1 teaspoon ground cumin
½ cup canned corn, drained (optional)

LIME CRÈME FRAÎCHE
1 cup sour cream
1 tablespoon fresh lime juice
Salt to taste
White pepper to taste

RED CHILE PESTO
2 dried ancho chiles
1 clove garlic
1 teaspoon ground cumin
1 teaspoon thyme
1 teaspoon dried basil
1 teaspoon Mexican oregano, or standard dried oregano
¼ teaspoon salt
3 tablespoons brandy
2 tablespoons water

10 corn husks, soaked in water for several hours (see Resources)
Red and blue corn chips

FOR THE ANASAZI BEAN FILLING, rinse beans under running water, then cover with 3 times as much water as you have beans. Soak overnight. Next day, drain beans, rinse again, and cover with fresh water in large saucepan. Add chicken base or bouillon and boil until beans are tender but not yet bursting, about 3 hours. (Note, boiling time may vary depending on freshness of beans.) Strain, gently rinse in cool water, and chill. Before serving, add onion, cilantro, peppers, green chiles, Tabasco, cayenne pepper, cumin, and corn (if desired). Stir to combine well. Reheat to warm through before assembly and serving.

FOR THE LIME CRÈME FRAÎCHE, whisk all ingredients together in small bowl. Taste and add more lime juice if desired. Refrigerate until needed.

FOR THE RED CHILE PESTO, soak the dried chiles in warm water until soft. Remove seeds and tear chiles into small pieces. Combine with all other ingredients in a blender and whirl until smooth. If the mixture is too wet, transfer to small heavy-bottomed saucepan and cook on medium-low heat to reduce slightly and thicken.

TO ASSEMBLE APPETIZER: Drain and pat dry the soaked corn husks with paper towels. Pull a ⅛- to ¼-inch strip from the edge of each husk to use as a tie; tie each cornhusk about ½ inch from each end to make a boat-like shape with a lengthwise opening. Put about ⅔ cup beans in each cornhusk boat. (If you have extra beans, reserve for another meal.) Top each with a dollop of Lime Crème Fraîche and on top of that a smaller dollop of Red Chile Pesto. You can make ahead to this point, and hold for a few hours until ready to heat and serve.

PLACE STUFFED CORNHUSKS on a baking sheet and heat in a 250-degree F oven before serving warm with red and blue corn chips for dipping.

BEANS

All cultures need a reliable source of protein to thrive, and in the Americas one primary source for millennia was beans. Beans are one of the oldest New World foods, originating probably in southern Mexico or Central America at least 7,000 years ago. When early European travelers arrived in the Southwest, they found Native peoples raising and storing impressive crops of beans, and were able to trade goods for the local food that helped them along their journeys.

Today, earthy-tasting, creamy refried pinto beans are a ubiquitous staple of Mexican restaurants. The beans are boiled until soft, mashed, and then fried in lard. In their dried state pintos are mottled beige and brown, but turn reddish brown when cooked. They are used classically in the Tostadas Compuestas (page 155). More recently, however, inventive restaurant chefs in the region have found ways to include other varieties of beans and cooking methods on their menus. Small black turtle beans, also called *frijoles negros,* have gained great popularity. They are not actually black but a very deep purple, which you will notice when some of the color leaches into the soaking water. Try them in the Black Bean Salad (page 109), the Black Bean Soup (page 77), or the Southwestern Succotash (page 207).

Unusual varieties of heirloom beans are also increasingly found in specialty stores and on plates in innovative restaurants. Among the most popular are the beautifully mottled burgundy and white variety called Anasazi, named after the Native Americans who lived in the Four Corners region until around the thirteenth century A.D. Similar in appearance are appaloosa beans. Try either of them in the Anasazi Bean-Dip Boats appetizer (page 51).

There are many other heirloom varieties that you can experiment with—the Seed Savers Exchange has a catalog of 1,500 varieties of beans, while the Native Seeds/SEARCH catalog lists fifteen exotic varieties, including Flor de Mayo (soft lavender from Mexico), Yellow Eye (mixed white and yellow from a Four Corners family farm), and Colorado River (maroon and cream). (See Resources, page 249, for source information on beans.) Other heirloom beans developed from Native American varieties include bolitas, a close relative of the pinto, and the tiny teparies, developed over generations by the Tohono O'odham people and adapted to grow in hot desert summers.

COOKING BEANS: One of the advantages of beans as a food is that they can be dried for long-term storage. That means that to become edible, they must be rehydrated, and that often takes time. You do this by covering them with cold water (at least one inch over the beans) and soaking for several hours or overnight, during which time they will take up water through the little "hilum"—the place at which each bean was attached to the pod. This will shorten the cooking time and also remove indigestible complex sugars, called oligosaccharides, that cause gas. By changing the soaking water several times and rinsing the beans before adding clean water, you will get even better results.

If you need to cook your beans quickly, you can use the quick-soak method. Use a large pot, because the beans will swell to three times their size. Cover the beans with plenty of cold, unsalted water. Bring to a boil over high heat for about 5 minutes. Then remove from the heat, cover, and let them soak for about 1 hour. Drain, rinse, and cover with fresh water to cook.

carnitas napoleon with green chile–tomatillo sauce

ATLAS BISTRO, PHOENIX, ARIZONA

MAKES 8 APPETIZER SERVINGS

Atlas Bistro's chef Carlos Manriques, who grew up in the border town of Mexicali, makes frequent trips to Mexico for renewed inspiration. This particular dish is a visually stunning starter for any dinner party. You can make the carnitas, sauce, and tortilla squares a day or two ahead, then warm everything just before you assemble and serve. If your ground red chile is on the hot side, you can eliminate the cayenne pepper. When roasting the meat, you'll need to insert something between the foil and the food, since the acid from the orange and Dr. Pepper will eat at the foil. Chefs typically use a kind of plastic wrap that can withstand higher temperatures than most brands you can buy in the grocery store; instead, use a sheet of parchment paper. And don't be concerned about the Dr. Pepper—somehow it all seems to work.

DRY RUB
2 tablespoons brown sugar
2 tablespoons ground red chile
1 teaspoon cayenne pepper
2 tablespoons dried garlic powder
1 teaspoon dried Mexican oregano, or standard dried oregano
1 teaspoon ground cumin
2 tablespoons kosher salt
¼ cup olive oil

CARNITAS
1 pound boneless pork shoulder meat, cut into large chunks and coated with dry rub
1 large orange, sliced into ¼-inch rounds with the rind on
1 large yellow onion, roughly chopped
1 cup Dr. Pepper soda

GREEN CHILE–TOMATILLO SAUCE
6–8 tomatillos
2 Anaheim chiles, roasted and peeled (see page 14)
3 medium cloves garlic
1 leek, cleaned and roughly chopped
2 cups chicken stock
1 cup lightly packed fresh cilantro leaves

TORTILLA SQUARES
6 corn tortillas
Vegetable oil

GARNISH
½ cup Terra Cotta Salsa Fresca (see page 221), or medium-hot store-bought salsa
3 tablespoons pomegranate seeds (optional)
3 tablespoons crumbled cotija (see page 22) or dry mild feta cheese
8 sprigs fresh cilantro

FOR THE DRY RUB, mix all ingredients together in a large bowl. Place pork chunks in this bowl and toss, coating pork generously. Cover, refrigerate, and let marinate overnight.

FOR THE CARNITAS, preheat the oven to 325 degrees F. In a large heavy frying pan brushed with oil, brown the pork over medium-high heat. Transfer to a heavy metal or ceramic baking pan that will fit the pork with room for orange, onion, and Dr. Pepper. Mix in the orange and onion, then pour Dr. Pepper over all. Cover the pork mixture tightly with sheet of parchment paper, then a sheet of foil. Cook for 3 hours. The carnitas should be so tender that the meat easily falls apart. Shred meat while still hot, using 2 forks.

FOR THE GREEN CHILE Tomatillo Sauce, husk and chop the tomatillos, discarding the hard stem ends. In a medium saucepan over low heat, combine the tomatillos with all other ingredients except for cilantro and simmer for about 30 minutes. Pick leaves off cilantro and discard stems. Set aside 4 sprigs for garnish. Combine cooked ingredients and cilantro in a blender and puree until smooth.

FOR THE TORTILLA SQUARES, trim tortillas into 2-inch squares, saving the scraps for another use such as baked or fried corn chips. You should be able to get 4 squares from each tortilla. Heat oil in a frying pan over medium heat. Fry the tortilla squares until crisp, turning with tongs, about 10–15 seconds. Drain on paper towels.

TO ASSEMBLE CARNITAS NAPOLEON: Place a tortilla square on a plate, topping with a small amount of warm carnitas (roasted pork). Stack with another chip and repeat until you have a tower of 3 layers. Pour Green Chile Tomatillo Sauce on top and drizzle around the edge of the plate. Finish with a small amount of Terra Cotta Salsa Fresca and a cilantro sprig, then sprinkle the plate with cotija and pomegranate seeds.

TOMATILLO

In Mexico the tomatillo is called *tomate verde,* which means "green tomato." However, tomatillos are not just small, under-ripe tomatoes, but a distinct vegetable in their own right.

The size of an apricot and covered with a papery husk, tomatillos are meatier but less juicy inside than a tomato. Tomatillos are an essential part of Mexican cuisine and have been since the Aztecs domesticated them.

Most tomatillos are harvested somewhat unripe, when then have a tart, slightly lemony flavor that adds zip to salsas. As they fully ripen they turn more golden in color and become sweeter.

To prepare tomatillos, first remove the husks and rinse off the sticky substance on the skin. Tomatillos are the main ingredient in classic salsa verde, which includes tomatillos, sliced green onions, green chiles, garlic, and cilantro. Salsa verde can be served raw or very lightly cooked. Carnitas Napoleon (page 55) includes a salsa verde.

Another classic and popular dish is pork stewed in tomatillo sauce. Cooked tomatillos lose some of their zip, so chefs frequently char or roast them to give them more depth of flavor. Roasted tomatillos are used in Navajo Eggplant (page 181) and Blackened Shrimp with Charbroiled Tomatillo Sauce (page 175).

Tomatillos are available in Hispanic markets and in many ordinary grocery stores. They are easy to grow, although they tend to sprawl. Harvest them when the fruit grows large enough to burst the husk. You can store ripe tomatillos still in their husks in the refrigerator for up to three weeks.

chile con queso

LA POSTA DE MESILLA, MESILLA, NEW MEXICO

MAKES 8 SERVINGS (ABOUT 2 CUPS)

The territorial-style La Posta Compound, which includes several shops as well as the original restaurant, is the on National Register of Historic Places. It is still run by the family of Katy Griggs Camuñez, who opened the restaurant in 1939. Chile con Queso makes an excellent dip for corn chips, or use as a sauce for steaks or burgers. The spiciness depends on the amount and hotness of the chiles. Although Velveeta cheese is currently in culinary disrepute, it is the classic ingredient for Chile con Queso—it melts easily and smoothly. Velveeta was introduced in 1929, and thus was almost the latest thing when La Posta opened ten years later. If you have no bacon drippings, you can substitute vegetable oil with a little loss of flavor.

2 tablespoons minced onion

1 tablespoon bacon drippings or vegetable oil

6–8 green Anaheim chiles, roasted, cleaned, and chopped (see page 14), or 1 can (7 ounces) chopped green chiles

1 large clove garlic, peeled and mashed

8-ounce package Velveeta cheese, cut in cubes

¼ pound longhorn or mild cheddar cheese, grated or cubed

⅓ cup half-and-half or canned condensed milk

USING A FRYING PAN large enough to hold the entire mixture, sauté the onion in your choice of fat over medium heat until translucent and soft. Then add chiles, mashed garlic, and the cheeses. Turn heat to low and stir frequently. When cheese is thoroughly melted, add half-and-half or canned milk and stir well. Do not allow the mixture to come to a boil. Serve warm.

garlic-sautéed lobster medallions with corn blinis and ancho crème fraîche

HEARTLINE CAFÉ, SEDONA, ARIZONA
MAKES 8–12 APPETIZER SERVINGS

The Heartline Café is regularly voted one of Sedona's best restaurants. Served in larger portions and with a green salad, this recipe could also be prepared as an excellent light lunch or supper. The ancho chiles give the crème fraîche an earthy chile flavor without much heat. If using frozen lobster, be careful in adding salt as the frozen lobster is packed in it. If lobster is unavailable, try large shrimp instead. For the roasted corn used in the blinis, you can roast a large ear of corn on a grill and then cut off the kernels, or you can use frozen or canned kernels and "roast" in a dry frying pan or wok over medium-low heat until brown.

CORN BLINIS
¾ cup roasted corn kernels (see recipe introduction)
1 tablespoon dry active yeast
6 ounces sour cream
2 egg yolks
1 teaspoon ground red chile
1½ cups flour
½ teaspoon salt
¼ cup sugar
About ¾ cup warm milk
2–3 tablespoons butter

ANCHO CRÈME FRAÎCHE
3–4 dry ancho chiles, soaked in warm water for 1 hour, seeds and stems removed
1 cup crème fraîche or sour cream
1 clove garlic, minced
Salt and pepper to taste

LOBSTER MEDALLIONS
1½–2 pounds of fresh or thawed frozen lobster meat (see recipe introduction)
¼ cup butter
1–2 cloves garlic, minced

¼ teaspoon dried thyme
Salt and pepper to taste

Chives or fresh thyme for garnish

TO MAKE BLINI BATTER, combine roasted corn kernels, yeast, sour cream, yolks, ground red chile, flour, salt, and sugar in medium bowl. Stir in milk, a little at a time, just enough to make a nonrunny batter. Set aside for 15 minutes to allow yeast to work. (While waiting, you can make the Ancho Crème Fraîche.)

MELT 2 TABLESPOONS of butter over low heat in a nonstick pan. Add tablespoon-sized scoops of blini batter to the pan and brown on each side to make cakes. Add more butter as needed as you fry the rest of the blinis. Cover with a clean kitchen towel and keep warm in very low oven.

TO MAKE ANCHO CRÈME FRAÎCHE, combine all ingredients in a blender or food processor until smooth. Refrigerate if making ahead.

FOR THE LOBSTER, slice lobster into thin medallions, about ¼-inch thick. Melt butter over medium-high heat, then add lobster, garlic, thyme, salt, and pepper. Sauté until lobster is just cooked, when it has turned opaque.

TO SERVE, put 1–2 tablespoons of Ancho Crème Fraîche on each plate and spread with the back of a spoon, set 2 or 3 blinis on the sauce, then distribute lobster on top. Garnish with a sprig of fresh thyme or chives.

habañero sea scallops
with southwest coleslaw

COYOTE GRILL, SCOTTSDALE, ARIZONA

MAKES 4 SERVINGS

These scallops and slaw are a fusion of flavors from two of the former Coyote Grill's most popular dishes. Remember to use gloves when preparing the habañero chile. Even if you can't handle the heat of a habañero, don't miss out on this dish. For softies, the pepper jack cheese may produce enough of a bite—just leave out the fiery habañero.

SOUTHWEST COLESLAW

4 cups finely shredded green cabbage

1 tablespoon minced chives

¼ cup julienned red bell pepper

¼ cup julienned green bell pepper

2 tablespoons olive oil

1½ teaspoons red wine vinegar

1 teaspoon honey

½ teaspoon salt

½ teaspoon black pepper

HABAÑERO PEPPER JACK SAUCE

1 cup heavy whipping cream

4 ounces shredded pepper jack cheese

¼–½ minced habañero chile

SCALLOPS

20 fresh or defrosted frozen sea scallops

2 tablespoons canola or other vegetable oil

2 tablespoons lemon juice

2 tablespoons white wine

1 teaspoon salt

1 teaspoon black pepper

FOR THE SOUTHWEST COLESLAW, mix all ingredients in a large mixing bowl until cabbage and peppers are evenly coated. Set aside. Refrigerate if making ahead.

FOR THE HABAÑERO PEPPER JACK SAUCE, combine all ingredients in a large saucepan and bring to a boil over high heat. Lower heat to a simmer and continue cooking until cream is reduced by half. If mixture is grainy, pour into a blender and blend until smooth. Keep warm.

SAUTÉ SEA SCALLOPS in oil, lemon juice, white wine, salt, and pepper until browned and firm. If liquids evaporate before scallops are done, add a splash or 2 of water.

MEANWHILE, to assemble, portion the Southwest Coleslaw on 4 plates, making flat nests. When scallops are nicely brown, remove using a slotted spoon and place 5 of them on each nest, then drizzle Habañero Pepper Jack Sauce over all.

oysters rio lobo with cilantro pesto

¡FUEGO!, TUCSON, ARIZONA
MAKES 4 SERVINGS

For years, ¡Fuego! has been the place to go in Tucson for fish. Chef-owner Alan Zeman is an expert in combining indigenous Southwestern ingredients into bright and unusual pairings. He is active in the Tucson culinary community and has won many awards from the public and his peers. This appetizer, which is colorful and full of flavor, has been on the ¡Fuego! menu for a long time and is a customer favorite. If you are able to choose your own oysters, pick those that are large and regularly shaped. If you can't find dried chorizo, try another hard sausage, such as pepperoni.

CILANTRO PESTO
1 cup lightly packed cilantro leaves
¼ cup freshly grated Parmesan cheese
2½ tablespoons unsalted, hulled pumpkin seeds
2–3 tablespoons olive oil
2½ teaspoons fresh lemon juice
2 large garlic cloves, chopped
¼ teaspoon salt

24 fresh oysters (in shells)

· 4 ounces dried Spanish chorizo, finely diced

1 poblano chile, roasted, peeled, and diced (see page 14)

1 red bell pepper, roasted, peeled, and diced (see page 14)

3 ounces Monterey Jack cheese, grated

4 cups multicolored dried beans

Sprinkle of ground red chile

1 lemon, quartered, with rind

1 lime, quartered, with rind

TO MAKE THE CILANTRO PESTO, combine all ingredients in a food processor bowl and blend until smooth, stopping to scrape down the sides of the bowl until everything is mixed. This may be made ahead and stored in the refrigerator for up to 4 days or freezer for 4 weeks.

TO MAKE THE OYSTERS, preheat the oven to 450 degrees F. Scrub oysters with a brush, removing all sand and any seaweed. Open oysters and place on half shell on a baking pan big enough to hold them all. Top each with ½ teaspoon pesto and portions of chorizo and the roasted chile and red bell pepper. Finish each oyster with a sprinkle of the Monterey Jack cheese. Bake for 8–10 minutes until oysters are just firm.

WHILE OYSTERS ARE BAKING, divide the dry beans among 4 wide, shallow bowls. When the oysters are done, arrange 6 oysters in each bowl. Sprinkle with ground red chile and put a lemon and lime wedge in each bowl. Serve immediately.

CITRUS

Christmas time in the Southwest finds many of our trees already naturally decorated with the brightly colored balls of oranges, tangerines, grapefruits, lemons, and limes. While citrus are not native to the region, they do well in the southern frost-free areas of Arizona, Texas, and California. Most citrus fruits begin ripening in late December, continuing on through late spring.

Although citrus used to be one of the so-called Four Cs driving Arizona commerce (along with cotton, copper, and climate), commercial production has declined somewhat in recent years as old groves have been uprooted for shopping centers and housing developments. But trees continue to flourish in the yards of homeowners and curbside in some of the older neighborhoods.

It is a particular joy to gather some oranges or a grapefruit, chilled by the long desert night, when you step out in the morning to pick up your newspaper. Should you be lucky enough to have a tree, use an orange or two in Baby Red Oak and Watermelon Salad with Orange Vinaigrette (page 117) or in Orange–Cranberry English Scones (page 37). And nothing is more convenient than easy access to a lime for a margarita or to a lemon when you need a few drops of juice to spark up a flat-tasting soup. Tangy fresh lime juice is used in the Pueblo Bonito Margarita (page 235), another beverage called the Rosalita (236), Lime–Cilantro Dressing (page 119), and Tequila and Citrus-Grilled Chicken (page 133). Lemons are called upon in Prickly Pear Lemonade (page 243) and will brighten the flavor of Chilled Tomato Bisque (page 85) and Habañero Sea Scallops (page 61).

Citrus trees are easy to grow, requiring only regular water, a well-positioned place in the sun, and the occasional dose of well-spaced fertilizer while the fruit is developing. New varieties are relatively disease free, taste sweeter, and have fewer seeds than older strains. One tree of each kind can provide plenty of fruit for a family and, as the trees mature, enough to share with the neighbors.

pueblo bonito guacamole

PUEBLO BONITO BED AND BREAKFAST INN, SANTA FE, NEW MEXICO
MAKES ABOUT 2 CUPS

Pueblo Bonito Bed and Breakfast Inn, just a stroll from downtown Santa Fe, was once a private estate with its own stables. The grounds still boast quiet courtyards, narrow brick paths, adobe archways to the street, and a shady garden sheltered by huge trees. Owners Amy and Herb Behm serve this guacamole to their guests in the late afternoon with blue-corn tortilla chips and chilled margaritas. Because avocados require a frost-free climate they do not grow in the Southwest, but as an essential element in Mexican cuisine, they are popular all over the region.

3 large, fully ripe avocados, peeled and pitted
1 tomato, seeded and finely diced
⅓ white onion, finely diced
1 fresh jalapeño chile, seeded and minced
3 medium cloves garlic, finely minced
Salt to taste
Fresh-ground black pepper (optional)
Juice of 3 limes or 2 lemons (about 2 tablespoons)

IN A LARGE MIXING BOWL, mash the avocados with a fork until mixture is smooth, but with a few chunks left for texture. Add tomato, onion, and chile, and mix thoroughly. Season with garlic, salt, and pepper to taste. Add the lime or lemon juice and mix well.

STORE CHILLED, but use within 2 hours of preparation. Let come to room temperature before serving.

rattlesnake empanadas

FURNACE CREEK INN, DEATH VALLEY NATIONAL PARK, CALIFORNIA

MAKES 16 EMPANADAS

To people unfamiliar with the desert, rattlesnakes and cacti are things to fear. But Furnace Creek Inn chef Michelle Hansen removes the threat and turns them into delicious appetizers for guests visiting Death Valley National Park. You can find canned rattlesnake meat in many gourmet stores or on the Web; you can also substitute chicken—and just tell people it's rattlesnake. Puff pastry is available frozen at most grocery stores.

½ pound boneless rattlesnake meat, or chicken
2½ tablespoons chicken fat or butter
¼ cup finely chopped red bell peppers
¼ cup finely chopped yellow bell peppers
¼ cup finely chopped green bell peppers
¼ cup diced nopalitos (prickly pear cactus pads, see page 72 and Resources)
1½ teaspoons ground cumin
½ teaspoon salt
½ teaspoon pepper
½ teaspoon powdered garlic
½ teaspoon ground red chile
2 tablespoons lime juice
2 defrosted puff pastry sheets
⅓ cup shredded Colby cheese
Egg wash (one egg, fork-whipped with 2 tablespoons water)

GARNISHES (OPTIONAL)
Terra Cotta Salsa Fresca (see page 211)
Pueblo Bonito Guacamole (see page 65)
Sour cream
Ranch dressing

IN A FOOD PROCESSOR or blender, grind rattlesnake meat and chicken fat together until it looks like ground pork. Sauté peppers, nopalitos, and ground meat together over medium heat for about 15 minutes. Add everything else to the skillet except the pastry, cheese, and egg wash. Cook for 5 minutes more. Drain if necessary and let cool. Add shredded cheese to mixture.

PREHEAT THE OVEN to 350 degrees F. Lightly flour a surface, spread out pastry sheets, and roll each to approximately 8 x 16 inches. Using a biscuit cutter, cookie cutter, or empty can, cut out 8 circles, 4 inches across, from each sheet. Place a tablespoon of the mixture in the middle of the circle, fold the pastry together, and crimp closed with fingers or fork. Place on a nonstick baking sheet and brush the pastry with egg wash. Bake for about 12 minutes until golden brown.

SERVE WITH your choice of garnishes.

black guajillo scallop tostadas

ATLAS BISTRO, SCOTTSDALE, ARIZONA
MAKES 10 APPETIZER SERVINGS

While this starter is definitely recognizable as a tostada, the flavors will transcend any tostada you've had before. Atlas Bistro chef Carlos Manriquez advises using local organic produce and English cucumber, which is sweeter than regular cuke. He also prefers Maui or other sweet onions. The recipe calls for the scallops to be cooked by the ceviche's lime juices, but you can also pre-cook them by sautéing two to three minutes on a side until just opaque. You can buy flat tostadas already fried, or fry fresh corn tortillas in light oil over high heat until crisp, about 1 minute, then drain and cool. Although this is served as an appetizer at Atlas, two tostadas make a great lunch.

SCALLOP CEVICHE
1 pound bay scallops
½ cup cilantro leaves
½ cup chopped English cucumber
2 tablespoons cracked black guajillo chile pieces (see Resources)
½ cup firm, crunchy diced avocado
Juice of 3 Key limes or other limes
Sea salt to taste
Cracked white pepper to taste

BLACK GUAJILLO SAUCE
3 dried black guajillo chiles, seeds removed (see Resources)
2 Roma tomatoes
½ onion
2 cloves garlic
2 ounces Kahlúa or other coffee liqueur
2 tablespoons chicken stock
1 cup mayonnaise
Sea salt to taste
Black pepper to taste

10 fried corn tortillas (see recipe introduction)
1 cup cotija cheese

FOR THE SCALLOP CEVICHE, mix all ingredients in a bowl and refrigerate for 4–6 hours (see recipe introduction).

FOR THE BLACK GUAJILLO SAUCE, soak the guajillo chiles in hot water for 20 minutes. Remove from water, and take out seeds and any ribs. Tear into small pieces. Cut the Roma tomatoes in half and grill them and the onion over coals, or over medium-high heat in a heavy frying pan lightly brushed with oil, until lightly browned, about 5–7 minutes. Combine with garlic, Kahlúa, and chicken stock in blender and process until smooth. Transfer the mixture to a small bowl and mix with 1 cup mayonnaise. Add salt and pepper if desired.

TO ASSEMBLE: On each fried tortilla, spread 2 tablespoons of Black Guajillo Sauce. Add ¼ cup Scallop Ceviche and top with a sprinkle of cotija cheese.

AVOCADOS

••••••••••••••••••••••

Avocados mashed into guacamole or sliced into salads are a standard on every menu in the Southwest serving Mexican food or a version of New Southwest cuisine. Their bland, silky richness combines well with green chiles, and by themselves they can elevate the most pedestrian sandwich. The Pueblo Bonito Guacamole (page 65) represents a classic use of this fruit. For a salad, check out the Southwest Roasted Pepper and Avocado Salad (page 113) or the Guadalupe Salad (page 116), in which the avocado is used in the dressing.

Avocados frequently appear as an ingredient in cooked food, as in the Tortilla Lasagna (page 193), or in a garnish, as in the Black Guajillo Scallop Tostadas (page 67) and the Monte Vista Tortilla Soup (page 93).

Despite its importance in the regional cuisine, this fruit is, ironically, not something that a Southwestern chef can order from a local farmer. Avocado trees, native to southern Mexico, grow only in semi-tropical areas. They don't do well in cold winters or very dry, hot summers, or alkaline soil.

Around 95 percent of commercial American avocados are grown in southern California, where the high humidity and average temperature of 70 degrees F are perfect for the trees. (The other 5 percent are grown in Florida.) A handful of small growers and some home gardeners in southern Texas manage to produce small crops, and there are around a dozen trees in the Phoenix area that talented gardeners with ideal microclimates have been able to coax to bearing age. The best avocados are the Haas variety, which have a tough, dark pebbly skin. Second best are the more smooth-skinned Fuerte.

While it is true that avocados are high in fat, their oil content is mono-unsaturated fat, high in oleic acid, which is proven to reduce LDL or "bad" cholesterol. They are also high in potassium and a slew of vitamins.

Avocados are rarely sold ready to eat in the grocery store, but will ripen off the tree when stored at room temperature. You won't have much luck trying to hasten an avocado to ripen—it's best to try to anticipate when you'll need them and purchase them at least three days in advance. Ripe avocados can be held in the refrigerator for a couple of days. Once cut, they darken unless coated with lemon or lime juice.

steamed dos equis clams

CAFÉ CENTRAL, EL PASO, TEXAS
MAKES 2 SERVINGS

In a town where clean jeans are appropriate for most events, Café Central is the place to get dressed up and go to for a night out on the town. It has a sleek, urban bistro feel and elegant Continental dishes, many with a Southwestern twist to them. It was in that spirit that chef Jacob T. Hallberg created this dish. The two "x"s in Dos Equis (XX), a favorite Mexican beer, are pronounced EK-ees. If the jalapeño you are using is quite hot, just half a chile may be enough for you.

2 tablespoons extra-virgin olive oil
½ medium onion, thinly sliced
½–1 jalapeño chile, thinly sliced
1 tablespoon chopped garlic
1 bottle Dos Equis Lager
1 cup diced Roma tomatoes
1 cup chicken broth
18 littleneck clams
2 tablespoons finely chopped cilantro

HEAT OLIVE OIL on medium-high in a wide saucepan or deep skillet with a lid until the oil starts to smoke slightly, about 2 minutes. Sauté the onion, jalapeño, and garlic just until the garlic starts to brown. Add beer and continue heating until reduced by half. Add black pepper, diced tomatoes, and chicken broth. Stir, then add clams. Cover and simmer until all or most of the clams open, about 5 minutes. Discard any unopened clams. Divide into 2 bowls and garnish with cilantro.

wild mushroom quesadilla

FURNACE CREEK INN, DEATH VALLEY NATIONAL PARK, CALIFORNIA

MAKES 4 SERVINGS

Chef Michelle "Mic" Hanson, who presides over the kitchen at the Furnace Creek Inn, says she knew at nine years old what she wanted to do, and has never looked back. She specializes in eclectic cuisine and incorporates, when she can, wild ingredients collected in a sustainable manner so as not to deplete the resource. Wild mushrooms are frequently found in the higher mountains in the Southwest, particularly during summer's rainy season. Poisonous species frequently look remarkably similar to edible varieties, however; foragers spend considerable time in the field to become experts in mushroom identification. The safer alternative is to buy wild varieties in a specialty grocery store or farmer's market. You might consider a mixture of oyster, morel, chanterelle, or porcini mushrooms. Round them out with some portobellos if you wish.

1 tablespoon butter
4 cups sliced assorted wild mushrooms
4 large flour tortillas
3 cups shredded smoked Gouda cheese

GARNISH
Pueblo Bonito Guacamole (see page 65)
Salsa of your choice (or see Terra Cotta Salsa Fresca, page 211)
¼ cup sour cream

HEAT BUTTER in a large frying pan over medium-high heat and sauté the mushrooms. Set aside and keep warm. Heat the tortillas on grill or individually on a griddle or large frying pan. Spread cheese evenly over all tortillas. Sprinkle with mushrooms and wait for the cheese to melt. Fold over one side of tortilla to the middle, then fold the opposite side to overlap the first fold (looks like a letter ready for mailing!). Slice the folded tortillas into quarters. Sprinkle with salsa and serve with your favorite guacamole and sour cream.

PRICKLY PEAR PADS (NOPALES)

The recognizable and unique shape of the prickly pear cactus—think green pancakes, upended and attached edge-to-edge in a random pattern—has become a defining motif of the Southwest. The pads or stems of the prickly pear are an important vegetable in Mexican cuisine. Mexicans call them *nopales,* or *nopalitos* when they are cut into small pieces. Two simple but classic Mexican dishes are nopalitos with scrambled eggs and nopalitos in chile sauce.

Although all prickly pear pads are edible, it is the tall *Opuntia ficus indica* and similar species that produce the best nopales. Generally, the tender new pads appear in the late spring and are ready to be picked when they are about the size of a man's hand. However, commercial cactus growers are able to manipulate the growing conditions so that you can find nopales in Latin American markets year-round. In central California, John Dicus grows organic nopales from a nearly thornless strain developed on the Yucatan Peninsula. Because he picks and ships on the same day, the pads remain fresh in your refrigerator for weeks (see Resources, page 249).

For generations, Mexicans have known that nopales are good for people with diabetes, and within the last few years, scientific studies have proven this folk remedy to be accurate. Just 100 grams a day of nopales—about two medium-sized pads—can regulate the blood sugar. They are also good for people who need to control their cholesterol. It is still somewhat unclear what it is that makes prickly pear pads such a wonder food, but researchers believe it is a combination of some gums and fibers that contribute to the blood cleansing.

Prickly pear pads have a mild flavor and can be eaten raw or cooked. See Sonoran Cactus Fries, page 73, and Rattlesnake Empanadas, page 66.

sonoran cactus fries
with black bean caramel gravy

COWBOY CLUB, SEDONA, ARIZONA

MAKES 4 SERVINGS

The Cowboy Club is located in the old Oak Creek Tavern, an original gathering place for Sedona's earliest settlers. Many Western movies were shot in the spectacular Oak Creek Canyon nearby, and when the day's filming wrapped up, the stars and production folks would gather here to enjoy the warm fire and hospitality found within the old walls. These quintessentially Arizona appetizers were devised by Lawrence McGrael, the executive chef at today's Cowboy Club. The recipe seems a bit odd, but trust the chef on this one. If you don't have water from cooking black beans, improvise by stirring a little instant black bean powder into water. (Dried instant beans are often available in health food stores, stocked with other dried soups.)

BLACK BEAN CARAMEL GRAVY

2 cups black water from cooking black beans (see recipe introduction)

½ cup brown sugar

1½ teaspoons balsamic vinegar

¾ teaspoon vanilla extract

1½ teaspoons Dijon mustard

Salt and pepper to taste

2 tablespoons cornstarch

2 tablespoons cold water

CACTUS FRIES

4 medium-size nopales (prickly pear cactus pads; see page 72)

1 cup buttermilk

1 tablespoon flour

2 tablespoons baking powder

½ cup cornstarch

1 tablespoon salt

2 tablespoons paprika

1 teaspoon white pepper

3 tablespoons powdered garlic

1 tablespoon sugar

3 cups vegetable oil

FOR THE BLACK BEAN CARAMEL GRAVY, combine all ingredients except cornstarch and cold water in a medium saucepan and bring to a boil over high heat. Turn down heat to medium. Combine the cornstarch with cold water, then add to the gravy, whisking as it thickens. If it appears to be too thick add a little more water and whisk until smooth.

FOR THE CACTUS FRIES, clean the nopales by scraping off the stickers and trimming the edges and tough stem end. Cut each pad into strips about ½-inch wide. Put the buttermilk in a shallow dish. Mix all other ingredients except oil in a second shallow dish. Dip each cactus strip in buttermilk, let most of it drain off, then dip it in the dry mixture. Heat oil to 325 degrees F. Cook cactus strips 2 or 3 at a time for about 3 minutes or until crispy. Remove with a slotted spoon and drain on paper towels.

SERVE WARM with Black Bean Caramel Gravy.

soups and stews

black bean soup

EL TOVAR LODGE, SOUTH RIM, GRAND CANYON, ARIZONA

MAKES 8 SERVINGS, ABOUT 1 CUP EACH

A World Heritage Site, the Grand Canyon is one of the most studied geologic land-scapes on Earth. It has been inhabited for centuries and contains evidence of the past in more than 2,600 prehistoric ruins. During summer, the area is crowded with visi-tors from many countries, but winter, with its occasional dusting of snow, brings a special beauty to the canyon. What a pleasure to savor this black bean soup in the comfortable dining room at El Tovar after a winter morning's hike along the canyon rim. Cook the beans in your crockpot for carefree preparation.

¾ pound black beans

2 tablespoons bacon fat or vegetable oil

1 onion, medium diced

1 garlic clove, minced

8 cups chicken stock

1 smoked ham hock

⅓ cup dry sherry

½ tablespoon ground red chile

¾ teaspoon ground cumin

1 tablespoon Tabasco

1 tablespoon red wine vinegar

½ teaspoon salt (optional)

⅛ teaspoon pepper

GARNISH

1 cup Lime Sour Cream (see page 168)

⅓ cup sliced green onions (sliced on the bias)

5 corn tortillas, cut in half, then into thin strips

SOAK BEANS overnight in enough cold water to cover them by 1 inch. Drain and rinse.

HEAT THE BACON FAT in a heavy 3-quart pot over medium-high heat; add the onions and sauté until translucent. Add garlic and sauté an additional 2 minutes, stirring constantly.

ADD THE CHICKEN STOCK and bring to a simmer, then turn the heat down. At this point you can transfer to a crockpot if you like. Add ham hock and beans, and simmer until the beans are tender, about 3 hours, depending on how fresh the beans are.

REMOVE THE HAM HOCK from the pot and let cool before cutting away any fat and dicing the meat into medium-size dice. Return the diced ham to the soup.

ADD THE REMAINING INGREDIENTS and continue to simmer for 20 minutes.

WORKING IN BATCHES of 2 cups at a time, puree the soup in a standard-size blender. (If you wish, save 2 cups of beans before pureeing and stir back into the soup after the rest is pureed to give the soup more texture.)

FOR TORTILLA STRIPS, preheat the oven to 325 degrees F. Bake the strips on an ungreased baking sheet for 8–10 minutes.

TO SERVE, ladle soup into individual bowls and garnish each with Lime Sour Cream, tortilla strips, and sliced green onions.

butternut squash soup with goat cheese ravioli and fried sage

GRAZE BY JENNIFER JAMES, ALBUQUERQUE, NEW MEXICO

MAKES 6–8 SERVINGS

Chef Jennifer James serves traditional American food in a romantic, casual setting. She operates two restaurants and in both, diners can choose to make a meal out of a number of small plates rather than order traditionally. James's menus are seasonal, rotating to feature whatever is best in local produce. This soup is a customer favorite, although it is not always available. The recipe calls for roasting the squash twice. This second roasting intensifies the flavor and the sweetness of the squash without adding extra sugar. Fresh wonton wrappers are used for the ravioli; they are usually found in the produce section.

BUTTERNUT SQUASH SOUP
1 large butternut squash (about 2½ pounds)

1 medium shallot, minced

1 medium garlic clove, minced

1 tablespoon canola oil

½ teaspoon cinnamon

½ teaspoon ground allspice

2½–3 ½ cups vegetable stock

Salt and pepper to taste

2 tablespoons heavy cream (optional)

GOAT CHEESE RAVIOLI
¼ cup (2 ounces) fresh creamy goat cheese

1 tablespoon heavy cream

Salt and pepper to taste

16 wonton wrappers

FRIED SAGE
12–18 fresh whole sage leaves

About ½ cup oil

FOR THE BUTTERNUT SQUASH SOUP, preheat the oven to 350 degrees F. Halve the squash and scoop the seeds out. Place flesh-side-down on an oiled baking sheet and bake until soft (your finger can make an indent in the skin), about 30–40 minutes. When it's cool enough to handle, scoop out the flesh until you have 2 cups of it, then return this portion to spread on the baking sheet. Reserve the remainder, if any, for another use and discard the skin.

ROAST THE SQUASH again at 250 degrees F, stirring occasionally, until it is mostly dry and its flavor has deepened, about 30 minutes.

MEANWHILE, IN A LARGE HEAVY STOCKPOT, cook the shallots and garlic in canola oil over medium-high heat until soft and caramelized. Stir in spices and cook 1–2 minutes, until the spices are fragrant.

ADD THE ROASTED SQUASH and vegetable stock and bring to simmer over medium-low heat; the liquid should just cover the squash. Continue simmering for about 15 minutes, then transfer in batches to a blender and puree.

ADJUST THE CONSISTENCY of the soup to your taste by adding more stock or cooking longer to reduce liquid. Season to taste with salt and pepper.

AFTER PUREEING, stir in 2 tablespoons of cream, if desired, to add a little richness.

FOR THE GOAT CHEESE RAVIOLI, while the squash is baking, stir the creamy goat cheese in a small bowl with cream, salt, and pepper. Lay 8 wonton wrappers on a baking sheet or other flat surface. Brush the wrapper edges with water. Scoop 1 teaspoon of the goat cheese mixture onto the center of each wrapper. Top each with a second wrapper, using your fingers to gently push air out of the ravioli. Seal the edges with a fork or ravioli maker.

IF YOU ARE MAKING RAVIOLI AHEAD, freeze them on baking sheet, about 1 hour, then place it in freezer bags; they can store for up to 2 months. When ready to use, do not thaw; place frozen ravioli in a pot of boiling water, reduce heat to a gentle roil, and cook until ravioli are soft, about 7 minutes.

TO COOK FRESH RAVIOLI immediately, bring a pot of water to a gentle simmer over medium heat. Add ravioli and cook until heated through, about 7 minutes.

FOR THE FRIED SAGE, gently rinse the sage leaves and pat dry. In a nonstick pan, heat oil over medium-high heat. When it's hot, carefully add the leaves (work in batches, if necessary) and flash-fry for about 5 seconds. Quickly remove with a slotted spoon to paper towels to drain.

TO SERVE, ladle soup into individual bowls; float 1 ravioli on the surface of each and top with 2–3 fried sage leaves.

SOUTHWEST SEASONINGS: THE THREE C'S AND AN E

Traditional herbs are essential for producing the definitive, sparkling flavors of Southwestern cuisine. Cilantro is used fresh, as the flavor disappears when it dries. It is usually sold in a small bunch tied with string. The others can be purchased dried and kept for several months.

CILANTRO

There aren't many people who feel neutral about cilantro—you either love or hate this stringent herb. And if you are not fond of the flavor, you'll find it difficult to avoid in Southwestern cuisine. Cilantro looks similar to flat-leaf parsley, a botanical relative. But it tastes and smells quite different, stronger and more distinct than parsley.

Cilantro is sometimes called Chinese parsley, Mexican parsley, or fresh coriander, as it is actually the fresh leaves of the coriander plant. It was grown in antiquity in southeastern Europe, Egypt, and China, spread first to the Caribbean islands, and then was brought to Mexico by the Spanish colonists.

Now it has become an almost ubiquitous Mexican seasoning—essential in salsas like Terra Cotta Salsa Fresca (page 211), Zion Pico de Gallo (page 211), El Tovar Fire-Roasted Corn Salsa (page 209), and Mango–Olive Salsa (page 210). It is also excellent in a salad dressing (Lime-Cilantro Dressing, page 119) and is often used with fish or in soups.

Cilantro is easy to grow. The bunches of cilantro sold in the grocery store usually contain more of the herb than is called for in any recipe, so it's convenient to grow your own and snip off just as much as you need.

CORIANDER

Whole coriander is in the shape of tiny balls. They appear to be seeds but are in fact the dried flowers of the coriander/cilantro plant. You can produce your own by letting your cilantro plants flower. When the flower parts have turned from green to brown, pluck and dry them, then store in airtight jars. To release the best flavor, toast coriander lightly in a dry frying pan, then crush in a mortar just as you're ready to use them. Gingery-tasting coriander flavors Sonoran Tortilla Soup (page 95), Pepper Picasso Soup (page 97), Tequila and Citrus-Grilled Chicken (page 133), and Goat Cheese-Stuffed Poblano Chiles (page 179).

CUMIN

The sharp, slightly bitter flavor of cumin is essential to the taste we expect from chile con carne, and cumin is often combined with chile in pre-packaged chili powders. It can be purchased ground or in the whole seed form that you can toast and grind yourself for more robust flavor. Cumin is a native of upper Egypt, where it has been cultivated since Biblical times. In Mexican groceries, it is often labeled *comino*.

Cumin also is frequently used in bean dishes such as Black Bean Soup (page 77), and in chile sauces such as the fresh tomato sauce in Canyon Ranch Grilled Chicken Enchiladas (page 128).

EPAZOTE

Epazote is traditionally used in the cuisines of southern Mexico. The name is derived from the Aztec word for the plant. Cookbook author Diana Kennedy calls it "the most Mexican of the culinary herbs." When tasted separately, the flavor is pungent—some say it tastes medicinal. Like cilantro, it is not universally relished, but it does impart a special flavor note to beans, especially black bean dishes. It's frequently used with beans because it contains compounds that reduce the gas that many bean dishes cause.

Although epazote is easy to grow, it's sometimes hard to find it in fresh form. The best bet is a Mexican grocery store; one teaspoon of dried epazote is the equivalent of about seven fresh leaves. Epazote is called for in the recipe for Stuffed Squash Blossoms (page 188).

carrot and ginger soup

LAMBERT'S OF TAOS, TAOS, NEW MEXICO

MAKES 8–10 SERVINGS

The secret of this soup is not to overcook the vegetables, otherwise the sweet carrot flavor will be overwhelmed by the spicy ginger. The pickled ginger called for is the same as the thin slices often served with sushi. Look for it in any market carrying Oriental products. It is not essential to include the pickled ginger, but it adds depth of flavor. Chef/owner Tina Lambert says, "This is a wonderfully simple and delicious soup that can be served chilled in the summer or hot for fall or holidays." If the soup is served chilled, it will thicken, so add more half-and-half to thin a little. For a vegan option, you may substitute all coconut milk for the half-and-half.

3 cups peeled and chopped carrots

1 cup chopped onion

½ cup peeled and chopped fresh ginger

2 tablespoons olive oil

¼ cup pickled ginger

5 cups water or chicken stock

1 cup half-and-half

1 cup canned coconut milk (optional)

Salt

White pepper

¼ cup toasted almond slivers

2 tablespoons chopped fresh chives

SAUTÉ THE CARROTS, onion, and fresh ginger in olive oil in a large heavy pot over medium heat for about 5 minutes. The vegetables should be soft, but not brown. Add the pickled ginger and chicken stock or water, bring to a boil, then reduce heat to low and simmer until the vegetables are just tender enough to puree, about 15 minutes.

TRANSFER THE SOUP to a blender and puree until smooth, working in batches if necessary. Return to the pot and add half-and-half and coconut milk, if desired, and stir to combine. Season to taste with salt and white pepper.

GARNISH SERVINGS with toasted almonds and chives.

chilled tomato bisque

ANTHONY'S IN THE CATALINAS, TUCSON, ARIZONA

MAKES 8 LARGE SERVINGS

Brian Triano, chef at Anthony's in the Catalinas, devised this soup to take advantage of the flavorful tomatoes grown in Willcox, Arizona. The soup has a sophisticated flavor, and with both cream cheese and heavy cream used, is velvety rich. You do not need to sieve the vegetables, as called for here, if you don't mind some healthful fiber in your soup.

3 pounds Roma tomatoes, chopped

1 large white onion, finely diced

4 tablespoons minced garlic

4 ribs celery, leaves removed, finely diced

2 cups ruby sherry (or substitute 1 cup dry sherry and 1 cup red wine)

4 ounces cream cheese, cubed, at room temperature

4 cups canned tomato juice

¼ cup sugar

1 teaspoon chopped fresh thyme

1 teaspoon chopped fresh tarragon

3 cups heavy cream

1½ teaspoons Tabasco

2 tablespoons lemon juice

Salt and pepper to taste

GARNISH

8 fresh lime wedges

8 tablespoons sour cream

SAUTÉ TOMATOES, onion, garlic, and celery in a deep heavy pot or large sauté pan over medium heat until the vegetables are translucent, about 10 minutes. Add sherry (and wine if using) and cream cheese and continue cooking until liquids are reduced by one-fourth. Remove from heat and puree in a blender, working in batches if necessary. If you want a very smooth soup, pass everything through a kitchen sieve at this point.

RETURN THE PUREE to the pot over medium heat and add tomato juice. Stir in sugar, fresh herbs, and heavy cream. Continue cooking, stirring occasionally, until liquids are again reduced and thickly coat the back of a spoon. Season with Tabasco, lemon juice, and salt and pepper. Remove from heat, cool, and chill for at least 1 hour. The soup will keep, refrigerated and tightly covered, for up to 3 days.

SERVE WITH FRESH LIME wedges and a dollop of sour cream.

cream of green chile soup

CAFÉ CENTRAL, EL PASO, TEXAS
MAKES ABOUT 6 SERVINGS, 1 CUP EACH

This recipe has been handed down through several decades of Café Central chefs. When planning to make this soup, you'll have to assess your own tolerance for *picante*. If you prefer milder chiles, make sure the Anaheims you purchase are a milder strain; otherwise you can substitute poblanos for some or all of the Anaheims. If the chiles you are using are spicy enough for you, you can eliminate the jalapeño.

2 medium yellow onions, chopped
6–8 minced garlic cloves
2 tablespoons olive oil plus 1 tablespoon butter
1 pound roasted and peeled green Anaheim chiles, chopped (about 2 pounds fresh)
1 jalapeño chile, minced (optional)
⅛ cup white wine
4 cups heavy cream
4 cups half-and-half
3 chicken bouillon cubes
1½ cups sour cream
White pepper
Salt to taste

IN A LARGE, heavy-bottomed pot, sauté onions and garlic in olive oil and butter over medium-high heat until softened. Add green chiles and jalapeño and continue to sauté until the chiles are tender and some browning has begun on the bottom of the pot. Add wine and scrape up browned bits with a wooden spoon. Continue cooking until the wine reduces to almost dry.

ADD HEAVY CREAM, half-and-half, and bouillon cubes. Let the mixture come to a boil, then reduce heat to low to allow a small simmer. After 45 minutes at low simmer, add sour cream, salt, and white pepper. Stir until the sour cream dissolves.

LET SIMMER another 10–15 minutes. Transfer to a blender and puree, working in batches if necessary. Pour the blended soup through a fine strainer and serve warm.

red bell pepper soup

CHRISTOPHER'S FERMIER BRASSERIE, PHOENIX, ARIZONA

MAKES 6–8 SERVINGS

Christopher Gross, the chef/owner of Christopher's Fermier Brasserie, trained in Europe and in top restaurants around the country before settling in the Southwest. The Brasserie features a fresh French-inspired menu using ingredients obtained from local and regional farms. This soup is extremely rich, silky, and flavorful. With little loss in quality, however, you can substitute whole milk for four cups of the cream and omit the butter for a less decadent version.

¼ cup olive oil
7 medium red bell peppers, in large dice
3 leeks, white part only, chopped
2 medium carrots, peeled and chopped
2 medium onions, chopped
7 cups chicken stock
2 potatoes, peeled and chopped
2 fresh thyme sprigs, or small pinch of dried thyme
1 bay leaf
6 cups heavy cream
1 tablespoon butter
Salt and fresh-ground white pepper

IN A HEAVY MEDIUM SAUCEPAN, heat 1 tablespoon of olive oil over medium-low heat. Add peppers, leeks, carrots, and onions, and sauté until softened, about 10 minutes. Add chicken stock, potatoes, thyme, and bay leaf. Increase heat to medium-high and simmer until the liquid is reduced by one-third, about 30 minutes. Remove thyme sprig and bay leaf. Working in batches, transfer the soup to a blender and puree. Strain the puree back into the saucepan, then add cream. Continue simmering about 15 minutes until the soup thickens to cream-like consistency.

REMOVE FROM HEAT and stir in the remaining olive oil. Finish with butter. Season with salt and white pepper and serve warm.

gazpacho float

HOUSE OF TRICKS, TEMPE, ARIZONA
MAKES 8 SERVINGS, ABOUT 1 CUP EACH

Robin and Robert Trick, chef/owners of the House of Tricks, have a reputation for offering their guests innovative dishes. Gazpacho has long been a Southwest favorite, but they give it a new twist with their mustard ice cream. The Tricks incorporate locally grown or produced ingredients in their dishes and change menu items frequently to reflect the availability of the freshest items.

GAZPACHO
2 cans (15 ounces each) stewed tomatoes, with juices
1 can (8 ounces) tomato juice
1 large cucumber, peeled, seeded, and roughly chopped
1 small yellow onion, peeled and roughly chopped
1 small red bell pepper, stemmed, seeds and veins removed, roughly chopped
3 cloves garlic, peeled and roughly chopped
Juice of 1 fresh lime
2 tablespoons chopped fresh basil
2 tablespoons chopped fresh mint
2 tablespoons chopped fresh cilantro
1½ teaspoons ground red chile
1 tablespoon balsamic vinegar
2 tablespoons kosher salt
2 tablespoons fresh-ground black pepper

HONEY-MUSTARD ICE CREAM
1 pint vanilla ice cream
2 tablespoons honey
1 tablespoon whole grain mustard

GARNISH
Fresh basil leaves

FOR THE GAZPACHO, combine all ingredients except salt and pepper in a large blender and puree until smooth. Season with kosher salt and black pepper to taste. The gazpacho should be made at least 2 days in advance of serving to give the flavors time to blend; tightly cover and store in the refrigerator.

TO MAKE THE HONEY-MUSTARD ICE CREAM, allow the vanilla ice cream to soften, but not melt, in a large mixing bowl. Fold in the honey and whole grain mustard until well combined. Return the ice cream to the freezer until ready to serve. The ice cream can be prepared up to 2 days in advance.

TO SERVE, divide chilled gazpacho among 8 large martini glasses, or other large wide-rim stemware, filling them about ¾ full. Using a small 1- to 2-ounce scoop, float ice cream on top of the gazpacho. Garnish each serving with a fresh basil leaf and serve immediately.

palace corn chowder

THE PALACE BAR, PRESCOTT, ARIZONA

MAKES 6–8 SERVINGS

The Palace Bar on Prescott's historic Whiskey Row is Arizona's oldest restaurant and saloon. The ornate bar was brought on ship from the East Coast around Cape Horn for the opening of the saloon in 1877. The bar was host to many famous early Westerners, including Wyatt and Virgil Earp and Doc Holliday before they went to Tombstone. During the big fire in July 1900 that destroyed much of Prescott, loyal patrons carried the wooden bar across the street to save it. Today you can have a drink there and a good meal as well.

3 cans (15 ounces each) corn, drained

10 slices bacon, diced

1½ tablespoons chopped garlic

1 cup diced onion

2 cups diced celery

1 cup flour

4 cups water

½ cup white wine

3 tablespoons chicken base or powdered chicken bouillon

2 baking potatoes, diced

3 cups heavy cream

¼ teaspoon Tabasco

¼ teaspoon Worcestershire sauce
¾ teaspoon dried thyme
¼ teaspoon pepper
A few tablespoons half-and-half or milk (optional)

PREHEAT THE OVEN to 350 degrees F. Spread the corn on a baking sheet and roast in the oven until just turning brown, about 8–10 minutes.

IN A LARGE STOCKPOT or heavy-bottomed saucepan, sauté the bacon and garlic over medium-high heat until the bacon is crisp. Remove bacon and garlic and reserve. Add onion and celery and continue sautéing until vegetables are translucent. Stir in flour to make a roux. When blended, add water and wine, reduce heat and bring to a slow boil. Stir in chicken base or bouillon, then add potatoes and roasted corn and continue cooking 15–20 minutes or until the potatoes are tender. Add cream, Tabasco, Worcestershire sauce, thyme, pepper, and reserved bacon and garlic, and stir well. Bring to a slow simmer again, stirring regularly so as not to burn. If the chowder seems too thick, add a little half-and-half or milk, about a tablespoon at a time, until desired consistency is achieved.

SERVE WARM.

shiner bock barbecue onion soup

ROARING FORK, SCOTTSDALE, ARIZONA
MAKES 6 SERVINGS

A favorite of locals and foodies alike, Roaring Fork has been awarded "The Best Upscale Campfire Cooking" by *Phoenix* magazine and described as "elevated cowboy food" by *Food and Wine* magazine. And while it's true this soup could well be made in a big cast-iron pot over an open campfire, fortunately it's just as good when you make it inside in your own kitchen. The chef suggests using a pinch of cayenne pepper to add a nice flavor profile to the finished soup. Any light, summer ale from your local microbrewery can be used in place of the Shiner Bock brand.

¾ cup chopped bacon
6 cups finely sliced yellow onions
1 teaspoon minced garlic
1 tablespoon finely chopped serrano chile (optional)
3 tablespoons butter
¼ cup flour
12 ounces Shiner Bock beer
4 cups veal stock (chicken broth may be substituted)
Kosher salt and cracked black pepper to taste
Pinch of cayenne pepper (optional)

RENDER THE BACON until it is crisp over medium-high heat in a moderately hot Dutch oven or saucepan with a heavy bottom. (Alternatively, you may use a deep skillet.) Reduce heat to medium-low, then add onions and cover. Cook until the onions are tender, 5–7 minutes. Uncover, then add garlic, serrano chile, and butter. Stir until the onions begin to caramelize, about 10 minutes.

ADD FLOUR, stirring to thicken, but do not allow the mixture to stick to the bottom of the pan; then add beer. Turn up heat, bring the mixture to a boil, and slowly add veal or chicken stock.

SEASON TO TASTE with salt and pepper. Continue cooking another 5–10 minutes to smooth out the flavor of the beer and thicken the soup. Stir in a pinch of cayenne pepper if desired, then serve warm.

monte vista tortilla soup

MONTE VISTA FIRE STATION, ALBUQUERQUE, NEW MEXICO
MAKES 8 GENEROUS SERVINGS

This restaurant resided for nearly twenty years in Albuquerque along the historic Route 66. The pueblo-style building was originally built as a fire station in 1936. Tortilla soup recipes offer a wide latitude for originality. This version, which lingers in memory even though the restaurant is now closed, is a little more elaborate than most, but absolutely delicious. The primary source of heat in the liquid is the habañero chile. Wear gloves when cutting and removing seeds from habañero. You need not leave it in for the full fifteen minutes; taste as you go along, and remove it when the broth is spicy enough for you.

8 cups chicken stock
1 can (28 ounces) whole peeled tomatoes with juices, or 2⅓ cups very thick tomato juice
1 clove garlic, chopped
¼ habañero chile, seeds removed
Salt and pepper to taste
1 dozen corn tortillas
¼ cup plus 1 tablespoon olive oil
2 chicken breasts, cut into 1-inch chunks
12 shrimp, peeled and deveined
3 red bell peppers, roasted (see page 14)
3 poblano chiles, roasted (see page 14)

CARAMELIZED ONIONS
2 red onions
2 tablespoons olive oil
2 tablespoons white wine
Salt and pepper to taste

GARNISH
2 avocados, peeled and sliced
½ cup fresh cilantro leaves
2 limes, quartered

BRING CHICKEN STOCK, whole peeled tomatoes, garlic, and the ¼ habañero to a boil in a large pot. Reduce heat to low and simmer for 15 minutes. Remove the habañero at this point unless you like it very hot! Transfer to a blender and puree, working in batches if necessary, then strain and return to the pot. Season with salt and pepper to taste, and keep warm.

FOR THE CARAMELIZED ONIONS, while the soup is simmering, peel the onions and cut them into thin strips. Sauté over high heat with 2 tablespoons olive oil, white wine, and salt and pepper until the onions are translucent. Turn heat down to medium or medium-low and let caramelize, about 15 minutes. The secret is to cook the onions very slowly so they do not brown or crisp, but become very soft and sweet.

WHILE THE ONIONS ARE COOKING, cut tortillas into ¼-inch strips. Heat ¼ cup oil over medium-high in a sauté pan; when ready add the tortilla strips in batches and fry until crispy, 10–15 seconds. Remove the strips from the oil and drain on paper towels. (These can be made ahead if you wish.)

HEAT 1 TABLESPOON OIL, and sauté the chicken over medium-high heat. When the chicken pieces are cooked through, about 2 minutes, add shrimp, roasted peppers, and caramelized onions.

WHEN THE SHRIMP TURNS PINK, remove the ingredients from the pan and place in the center of a large tureen, or divide among individual soup bowls. Pour in the soup stock. Garnish with sliced avocado, tortilla strips, cilantro, and lime wedges.

sonoran tortilla soup with machaca beef

TONTO BAR AND GRILL, CAVE CREEK, ARIZONA
MAKES 6–8 SERVINGS

Metropolitan Phoenix is as modern as tomorrow, but there are still a few corners that hearken back to its Old West past. Western-themed Tonto Bar and Grill sits on the original site of Rancho Mañana Dude Ranch, built in the early 1940s in the foothills north of Phoenix. Guests can dine inside or on one of the numerous patios. This is a very different tortilla soup from the Monte Vista version (see page 93). Here Chef Smith incorporates the tortillas as a thickening agent. This is a hearty soup that, with a salad, makes a satisfying dinner.

1 tablespoon oil
¾ pound beef (top or bottom round), cut into large chunks
1 yellow onion, diced
2 ribs celery, diced
3 medium tomatoes, chopped
2 tablespoons minced garlic
1 dried New Mexico or guajillo red chile, crushed and seeds removed
1 teaspoon black pepper
1 teaspoon kosher salt
1 teaspoon ground cumin
1 teaspoon ground coriander
1 teaspoon paprika
1 teaspoon ground red chile
6 cups chicken stock
8 corn tortillas
2 cups canola oil
1 roasted red bell pepper (see page 14), chopped
½ cup chopped cilantro
2 green onions, thinly sliced, for garnish

IN A MEDIUM POT with heavy bottom, heat oil over medium-high heat; add the beef and cook until well-browned. Remove beef with a slotted spoon and set aside.

IN THE SAME POT, add onions and celery and sauté until partially translucent. Then add tomatoes, garlic, dried chile, all spices, and chicken stock. Bring to a boil and add the cooked beef. Turn heat to low, cover, and simmer with the lid on for 1 hour.

REMOVE THE BEEF and set aside to cool. Keep the soup covered and gently simmering over low heat.

CUT 2 OF THE TORTILLAS into thin strips. Heat the 2 cups of oil in a heavy frying pan to around 350 degrees F. Drop in the tortilla strips and fry, about 10–15 seconds, then drain on paper towels and set aside. Fry the remaining tortillas whole and drain. When the whole tortillas are cool, break them into small pieces.

ADD THE CRUMBLED TORTILLAS to the simmering soup. When the tortillas are soft, carefully transfer the soup to a blender and puree, working in batches. Return the puree to the pot and continue cooking uncovered until thickened.

MEANWHILE, shred the cooled beef and add it to the thickened soup. Stir in roasted red pepper and cilantro just before serving.

GARNISH WITH fried tortilla strips and green onions.

pepper picasso soup

GHINI'S FRENCH CAFFE, TUCSON, ARIZONA
MAKES 6 SERVINGS

Coralie Satta-Williams is the chef-owner of Ghini's French Caffe. She calls her Pepper Picasso Soup "a soup that is a masterpiece in your mouth." She also has professional advice for home cooks: "The secret to every good recipe is first reading the instructions thoroughly and second *mis en place* ('everything in its place'), that is, prepare and measure everything out before beginning your recipe." The spiciness of the soup will depend on how hot your green chiles are. Chef Satta-Williams serves this with crusty French baguettes.

3 bell peppers (red, green, or mixed), seeded and chopped
¼ cup olive oil
½ cup chopped yellow onion
1 tablespoon chopped garlic
5 cups water
8 ounces roasted, peeled green chiles (canned or fresh)
1 teaspoon salt
1¼ cups half-and-half
¼ teaspoon paprika
¼ teaspoon ground coriander
¼ teaspoon black pepper
⅛ teaspoon cayenne pepper

FLOUR SLURRY
1 cup cold water
⅓ cup flour

GARNISH
½ cup plain yogurt
1 lime, cut in wedges

SAUTÉ PEPPERS in a dry preheated pan over medium heat until their skin starts to blacken. Transfer to a heavy-bottomed stockpot. Add olive oil, onion, and garlic, and continue cooking until the onions become golden. Add water, followed by remaining ingredients. At this point you must watch carefully so that the half-and-half doesn't cause the soup to curdle: Just as it comes to a boil, immediately reduce heat to low and simmer for 20 minutes.

CAREFULLY TRANSFER TO A BLENDER and blend until smooth, working in batches. Return the blended soup to the stockpot and reheat over low heat.

TO MAKE THE FLOUR SLURRY, mix cold water with flour in a jar, close tightly, and shake well to combine. Add the slurry to the heated soup and cook for 10 minutes on medium heat, or until the soup thickens and the flour is cooked.

GARNISH EACH individual serving with a dollop of plain yogurt and a wedge of lime.

gypsy stew

Rosalea Murphy, the founder and owner of the Pink Adobe, got this recipe from Vincente Romero, a flamenco dancer who discovered it (minus the chiles) while traveling with gypsies in Spain. New Mexican chile dishes are usually very spicy, and this recipe as presented here is no exception. If you prefer more moderate spiciness, you can still enjoy the excellent flavor of this dish by eliminating the jalapeño and yellow chiles and making sure the green chiles you use are mild. The Pink Adobe chefs warn that adding too much water will make your soup bland.

1 whole chicken (3–4 pounds)
2 cups cooking sherry
2 onions, chopped
3–4 garlic cloves, minced
Water
1 can (28 ounces) whole tomatoes (broken, with juice)
1 jalapeño chile, minced, seeds removed
16 ounces roasted fresh or canned whole green chiles (cut into 1-inch squares)
3 yellow torrido chiles (from a jar, seeds removed, cut into 1-inch squares)
Salt
8 cubes (1 inch square) Monterey Jack cheese

RINSE CHICKEN and remove any parts from the cavity. In a soup pot, combine the whole chicken, 1 cup of the sherry, onions, garlic, and just enough water to cover the chicken. Bring this to a boil, then turn down heat to low and simmer, covered, for about 1 hour or until the chicken is cooked. Remove from heat, then remove the chicken, leaving the broth in the pot, and let the chicken cool so that you can pick the meat off the bones. Discard skin and bone.

CUT THE MEAT INTO CHUNKS. Return the chicken to the broth and add remaining cup of sherry, tomatoes, and all chiles. Salt to taste. Reheat the stew over low until hot. Place cubes of Monterey Jack cheese in individual bowls and ladle stew on top.

maria's new mexican green chile stew

MARIA'S NEW MEXICAN KITCHEN, SANTA FE, NEW MEXICO
MAKES 8 SERVINGS

Laurie and Al Lucero took over the venerable Maria's (from Maria, of course) in 1985 and have endeavored to keep the authentic old New Mexico atmosphere. As for this recipe, one of the originals, Al says, "As with any recipe using local produce, the flavor and, in this case, the piquant nature of the chile, will vary, so tweak the recipe to your own taste by adding or reducing the amount used." There is a really high proportion of chile to other ingredients in this recipe, so feel free to use half the amount if you wish. Even at that, it is not a recipe for anybody not a dyed-in-the-wool chile-eater. Canned tomatoes work fine, and frozen New Mexico green chile may be substituted for fresh. Flour tortillas are the best accompaniment.

1 tablespoon shortening or cooking oil
3 cups cubed lean pork (about 1¾ pounds, cut into ¾-inch cubes)
4 potatoes, peeled and cut into 1-inch cubes
16 cups water
1 medium yellow onion, diced
4 cups whole, roasted, and peeled green chiles, stems removed (see page
14 and introduction to this recipe)
2 cups slightly crushed peeled tomatoes, canned or fresh, with juices
3 cloves garlic, minced
1 teaspoon salt or to taste
1 teaspoon flour

HEAT THE SHORTENING or cooking oil in a large frying pan over medium-high heat; add pork and sauté until slightly golden, about 2 minutes. Set aside.

RINSE THE POTATOES in cold water. Put them and 16 cups water in a 6–8 quart saucepan or stock pot and bring to boil. Continue boiling for 10 minutes, then add onion, chiles, tomatoes, garlic, and salt; lower heat to a simmer. Continue to simmer for about 30 minutes, uncovered, then add the pork and simmer for at least another half-hour. Add flour to thicken the broth, if desired.

SERVE IN LARGE BOWLS with plenty of broth.

the shed posole

THE SHED, SANTA FE, NEW MEXICO
MAKES 6–8 SERVINGS

Santa Fe locals and tourists alike have been flocking to The Shed since 1953, when it opened in a charming hacienda that dates back to 1692. The lovely patio in front provides a pleasant place to rest and is a buffer from busy Palace Avenue. Posole, a hearty corn and pork stew, is a traditional winter holiday dish in New Mexico, but the Carswell family, which runs The Shed, found it to be so popular, they added it to their regular menu. This recipe calls for dried hominy, but if you buy partially cooked hominy, usually found in the butcher section of the grocery store, you can skip the soaking and the cooking time will be shorter. If you wish to make your own red chile sauce, use the Tostadas Compuestas sauce recipe on page 154.

2 cups dry hominy (also called posole or nixtamal)
8 cups water, plus more for cooking
4 dried Anaheim chile pods
1 pound lean pork shoulder, cut into several large chunks
Juice of 1 lime
3 cloves garlic, minced
¼ teaspoon oregano
3 teaspoons salt (or to taste)

GARNISHES (OPTIONAL)
Chopped cilantro
Thinly sliced radishes
Lime wedges
Dried oregano
Red Chile Sauce (see page 154)

IN A MEDIUM BOWL, place the hominy and 8 cups of water. Soak overnight. If weather is hot, refrigerate. Drain the water and set the hominy aside. If using partially cooked or other prepared hominy, follow package directions.

BREAK THE DRIED CHILE PODS into small pieces and discard the seeds.

IN A LARGE HEAVY POT, combine the pork, hominy, lime juice, and chile pods. Add enough water just to cover the ingredients. Bring to a boil, then cover and turn heat down to low. Simmer for 3 hours, or until the hominy pops open. Add more water as needed, always keeping the ingredients covered. Stir occasionally.

REMOVE THE PORK, shred it, and return it to the pot. Add garlic, oregano, and salt. Simmer, covered, for 30 minutes more. Serve in large bowls. This dish can be accompanied by small condiment dishes of chopped cilantro, thinly sliced radishes, lime wedges, dried oregano, and red chile sauce.

MANGOS

The silken texture and luscious tropical flavor of mangos are a current hit with professional chefs. Ripe mangos go well with any type of seafood, and the fragrance and flavor evoke a feeling of the tropics, be it Mexico or the Caribbean.

Although mangos are available year-round, they are best during their peak season from early spring through late summer. There are actually more mango varieties in the world than there are apples, but only a few of these are available commercially. Not all mangos are labeled with their variety, but some of the best are Hayden, a smallish mango with yellow skin and red cheeks, and Keitt and Kent, both of which are rather large varieties with green skin and reddish cheeks. As with all fruit, try to buy mangos at their peak of ripeness—they will give slightly if you hold them in the palm of your hand. Mangos picked too green will eventually soften but won't develop the juicy sweetness that you want.

An easy way to transform a mango from whole fruit to a bowl of nice orange chunks is to slice it lengthwise, along the large, flat seed (place your knife about ¼ inch from the stem). Then score each half of fruit into dice-sized squares. Push the skin so the curve moves inside, and the mango squares will pop up, ready to be sliced off and used in your recipe. You will find mangos used in Flash-Grilled Ahi Tuna with Mango Relish (page 171), Pima Yellow Watermelon Soup with Ahi Ceviche (page 103), and Mango–Olive Salsa (page 210).

pima yellow watermelon soup with ahi ceviche, mango, and mint

KAI AT SHERATON WILD HORSE PASS RESORT & SPA, CHANDLER, ARIZONA
MAKES 6–8 SERVINGS

The Sheraton Wild Horse Pass Resort & Spa, Arizona's only Native American-owned luxury resort, is located on 1,600 acres of the 372,000-acre Gila River Indian Reservation. The architecture, design, art, and legends of the Pima and Maricopa tribes are celebrated throughout the hotel. Kai, the resort's signature restaurant, takes its name from the Pima word for "seed." The word has great relevance to the people of the Gila River Indian Community: It represents a connection to their past, their reverence for all of nature, and the belief that the land provides them with everything they need. Chef de cuisine Sandy Garcia, a member of the San Juan Pueblo Tribe in New Mexico, makes this soup with watermelons traditionally grown by the inhabitants of this lush high desert region. Much of the produce Chef Garcia serves comes from the Gila River Indian Community with its more than 35,000 acres of farms growing citrus, pistachios, olives, melons, and vegetables, and even aqua farms providing striped bass and other seafood.

WATERMELON BROTH
1 English cucumber, seeds removed
2 pounds yellow watermelon pulp, seeds removed
1 cup fresh lime juice

AHI CEVICHE
1 pound fresh ahi tuna, diced small
1 tablespoon grated fresh ginger
1 tablespoon finely chopped chives
2 tablespoons coarsely chopped cilantro
2 tablespoons coarsely chopped mint
1 ripe mango, diced small
½ cup ripe cantaloupe, diced small
¼ cup orange juice
¼ cup pink grapefruit juice
Juice of 2 limes
1 tablespoon sugar

Salt and pepper
8 fresh grapefruit sections

FOR THE WATERMELON BROTH, peel the cucumber and chop coarsely. Puree the watermelon and cucumber together in a blender. Add lime juice and blend in. Refrigerate while you make the ceviche.

FOR THE AHI TUNA CEVICHE, in a medium bowl, gently toss the tuna, ginger, chives, cilantro, mint, mango, and cantaloupe. Mix the juices and sugar in a cup, and pour over the ahi mixture. Season with salt and pepper.

LET MARINATE for 15–20 minutes. Drain and discard the marinade.

PREPARE THE GRAPEFRUIT SECTIONS by cutting the peel from the grapefruit with a small, sharp knife. Cut out 8 sections by cutting between the membranes and freeing the fruit. Hold aside in a bowl.

TO SERVE, using a small mold such as a ramekin or custard cup, pack ceviche into the mold, then upend into a shallow 8-ounce soup bowl. Repeat, making 6 or 8 servings. Pour melon soup into each bowl around the ceviche mound, garnish with a grapefruit section, and serve immediately.

salads

apple curry salad

SIMPLY DELICIOUS CATERING, FLAGSTAFF, ARIZONA

MAKES 6 SERVINGS

Nancy McCulla is a popular caterer in the northern Arizona town of Flagstaff. She formerly did catering for film shoots in the region and one night didn't get back to her kitchen until 3 a.m., after cooking "for days and days" in beautiful Monument Valley. She was ravenous, so, while others might have just eaten a few crackers and gone to bed, Nancy raided her cooler and, using just what she found there, devised this salad for herself. It has since become her most requested recipe. The dressing also makes an excellent marinade for chicken or can be brushed on fish while it is grilling. It will keep for a week in the refrigerator.

DRESSING

1½ tablespoons garlic puree

2 tablespoons minced shallots

2 tablespoons curry powder

¼ cup packed brown sugar

½ cup apple cider vinegar

1½ cups fresh apple cider

2 tablespoons strong mustard, such as stone-ground

1 cup applesauce

2¼ cups cold-pressed safflower oil or other light vegetable oil

½ cup extra-virgin olive oil

Kosher salt to taste

Fresh-ground black pepper to taste

SALAD

⅓ large red onion

1 Gala apple

6 cups baby spinach, or half spinach and half spring mix

¼ cup grated smoked gouda

1 cup toasted piñon nuts

FOR THE DRESSING, combine all ingredients, except oils and salt and pepper, in a food processor or blender until the mixture is well combined. Drizzle in oils until emulsified and thick. Season with salt and pepper. Transfer to a jar and store in the refrigerator if making ahead.

FOR THE SALAD, slice the red onion and apple into thin crescents. Combine the greens, gouda, and onion in a salad bowl and toss with dressing, reserving some for the apples. Dress apples in a separate bowl, then arrange them around the edge of the salad. Sprinkle piñon nuts on top.

PIÑON NUTS

Piñon nuts (or pine nuts) are produced in the cones of the piñon (also spelled pinyon) pine tree. These bushy trees thrive in the semiarid climate of the Southwest, growing on rocky foothills and mountain slopes from 4,500 to 9,000 feet in elevation. The slow-growing dark green trees even do well on steep sloping canyon walls.

Piñon pines produce a good crop of nuts only every three to six years, making them rather costly. You can legally collect them for personal use in national forests, but the labor involved is such that nuts already harvested can look like a bargain. Pine nuts imported from China and Italy (where they are called *pignolias*) are usually less expensive than those native to the Southwest.

Piñon nuts are 50 percent fat, and a single tiny nut can contain 20 calories; a mere pound of piñons supplies 3,000 calories! While this may be a problem for us in the twenty-first century, it was an important source of nutrition for Native Americans who were trying to survive on wild foods alone thousands of years ago. The Havasupai Indians who live at the bottom of the Grand Canyon formerly ground it fine for baby food.

Today we include piñons and their faintly resinous richness in everything from salads (Chicken Chopped Salad, page 111) to main dishes (Goat Cheese-Stuffed Poblano Chiles, page 179) or desserts (New Mexican Apple Pie, page 219).

The high fat content can cause piñon nuts to go rancid quickly. Store them in the refrigerator for three months; freeze them for longer storage and use within a year.

black bean salad

PASTICHE MODERN EATERY, TUCSON, ARIZONA
MAKES 8 SERVINGS

The word "pastiche" often defines an artistic composition made up of bits and pieces. That perfectly describes the menu at this cool and elegant restaurant. It also defines this salad—which also works well as a vegetable side dish for dinner. Pastiche chef Don Kishensky serves it with his Pastiche Salmon Cakes (see page 164). Although this salad is delicious enough for guests, it's easily put together with ingredients you probably have on hand, so don't be surprised if it becomes a standby for family rush nights.

2 cans black beans, drained and rinsed
½ cup diced red onions
2 ribs celery, diced
½ bunch cilantro, chopped
½ cup fresh lime juice
1 teaspoon minced garlic
2 tablespoons vegetable oil
1 tablespoon ground cumin
1 teaspoon pepper
1 medium tomato, diced
2 tablespoons sugar
1 teaspoon salt

COMBINE ALL INGREDIENTS in a large bowl. Serve with a slotted spoon.

broccoli–mushroom salad with orange–sesame dressing

FOUR AND TWENTY BLACKBIRDS, SANTA FE, NEW MEXICO

MAKES 4 ENTRÉE SERVINGS (1 CUP EACH) OR 8 SIDE SERVINGS

Four and Twenty Blackbirds is a restaurant with a country-store ambiance that echoes the original Griego Grocery Store, operated on the same site for sixty years. Proprietor Jo Ellen Thompson says, "Unlike most broccoli salads, this is not overwhelmed with creamy sweetness, but is instead a healthy alternative." She invites you to stop in for lunch or simply to browse and say "Hi!" on your stroll along the Old Santa Fe Trail.

ORANGE-SESAME DRESSING

⅓ cup orange juice

3 tablespoons sesame oil

1½ tablespoons tamari or soy sauce

2 tablespoons toasted sesame seeds

½ teaspoon salt

½ teaspoon pepper

SALAD

2 cups bite-size broccoli floret pieces

½ cup coarsely chopped pecans

1½ cups sliced mushrooms

½ cup dried cranberries

2 tablespoons minced red onion

4 cups mixed greens

FOR DRESSING, combine all ingredients in a jar and shake to blend well.

COMBINE BROCCOLI, pecans, mushrooms, cranberries, and red onion in a bowl and toss with dressing. Divide the greens among 4 plates. Pile the broccoli salad high on top of the greens and serve.

chicken chopped salad with baby romas and gorgonzola vinaigrette

NORTH MODERN ITALIAN RESTAURANT, TUCSON, ARIZONA

MAKES 4 SERVINGS

North, located in an upscale shopping center in Tucson's Santa Catalina Mountains foothills, has been a hit since the night it opened. The menu includes numerous substantial salads like this one. Piñon nuts are as Italian as they are Southwestern. Lightly toasting the piñon nuts first in a dry skillet enhances their flavor.

SALAD
12 ounces chicken breasts (2 medium boneless breasts)
2 tablespoons olive oil
Salt and pepper to taste
12 ounces of mixed baby greens (7–8 cups)
20 baby Roma, grape, or pear tomatoes, sliced in half

DRESSING
3½ tablespoons lemon juice
2 tablespoons red wine vinegar
1½ ounces Gorgonzola cheese, crumbled
½ cup extra-virgin olive oil
½ teaspoon sea salt
Pinch of white pepper

GARNISH
4 tablespoons crumbled Gorgonzola cheese
4 tablespoons toasted piñon nuts

PREHEAT THE OVEN to 375 degrees F. Lightly coat the chicken breasts with olive oil and season with salt and pepper. Bake uncovered for 12–15 minutes or until juice runs clear. When cool, pull the chicken apart into bite-size pieces.

FOR THE DRESSING, using a food processor, blender, or wire whisk, blend the lemon juice and wine vinegar with Gorgonzola until creamy. Slowly add the olive oil in a thin stream until emulsification occurs. Add salt and pepper and adjust for taste.

PUT THE MIXED BABY GREENS, chicken, and tomatoes in a bowl and toss with ¾ cup of the dressing; add more dressing to your taste. The remainder can be stored in the refrigerator for up to 1 week and is good on any salad. Arrange salad onto 4 plates and garnish each plate with Gorgonzola and piñon nuts.

chicken salad with cranberry vinaigrette

CASA SEDONA BED AND BREAKFAST INN, SEDONA, ARIZONA

MAKES 8 SERVINGS

Casa Sedona, with its lush flower gardens and juniper-scented air, has been named one of the top romantic inns in North America. Guests can enjoy the sight of the soaring red-rock cliffs from throughout the resort. Owner Donna Marriott has made this salad when hosting gatherings of the Sedona Chamber of Commerce and other bed-and-breakfast owners.

CHICKEN SALAD
4 cups diced cooked chicken
1 cup chopped celery
½ cup mayonnaise
½ cup sour cream
2 cups green seedless grapes
½ teaspoon salt
½ teaspoon pepper
½ cup chopped pecans
1 head leaf lettuce, washed and dried

CRANBERRY VINAIGRETTE
¾ cup olive oil
¼ cup red wine vinegar
1 teaspoon salt
1 teaspoon sugar
½ teaspoon pepper
½ teaspoon paprika
¼ teaspoon dry mustard
½ cup canned whole-berry cranberry sauce

FOR THE CHICKEN SALAD, mix all ingredients, except the lettuce, in a medium bowl, cover tightly, and refrigerate overnight or until ready to serve.

FOR THE CRANBERRY VINAIGRETTE, process all the ingredients in a blender until smooth. Refrigerate until ready to use (or up to 1 week).

AT SERVING TIME, line individual plates with lettuce, top with a portion of chicken salad, and pour dressing over all.

southwest roasted pepper and avocado salad with pineapple vinaigrette

CANYON RANCH, TUCSON, ARIZONA
MAKES 4 SERVINGS

The Southwest Roasted Red Pepper and Avocado Salad is refreshing and fun to eat. The salad ingredients are fairly simple but, for further ease of preparation, you can use roasted red peppers from a jar. What really makes this recipe is the pineapple vinaigrette—you won't even notice that it's lowfat.

PINEAPPLE VINAIGRETTE
¼ cup frozen pineapple juice concentrate
3 tablespoons Champagne vinegar
1 tablespoon olive oil
¼ teaspoon salt
Pinch of black pepper
1½ teaspoons chopped fresh mint

TORTILLA CHIPS
1 small flour tortilla, about 6 inches in diameter
Pinch of dried garlic
Pinch of ground red chile
Pinch of cumin seed
Pinch of salt

4 ounces organic spinach, thinly sliced, about 2 cups
4 ounces Romaine lettuce, thinly sliced, about 2 cups
¼ cup thinly sliced red onion
1 small Roma tomato, thinly sliced
½ red bell pepper, roasted and thinly sliced (see page 14)
½ yellow bell pepper, roasted and thinly sliced (see page 14)
½ avocado, mashed

FOR THE PINEAPPLE VINAIGRETTE, combine all ingredients in a blender and mix well.

PREHEAT THE OVEN to 350 degrees F. Slice the tortilla into 8 bite-size chips. Place on a baking sheet and sprinkle with seasonings. Bake for 3–5 minutes or until chips are golden-brown.

IN A LARGE BOWL, combine the spinach, romaine lettuce, onion, and tomato. Add pineapple vinaigrette and mix well.

DIVIDE INTO 4 PORTIONS and place on salad plates. Arrange 1 tablespoon each of roasted red and yellow peppers over the greens and top with 1 tablespoon of mashed avocado. Garnish with 2 tortilla chips.

green-apple–celery-root slaw
with tarragon vinaigrette

BRITTLEBUSH BAR & GRILL, WESTIN KIERLAND RESORT & SPA, SCOTTSDALE, ARIZONA

MAKES 8–10 SIDE SERVINGS

The Southwest's warm winter weather frequently makes salad a good choice for lunch, although some salad ingredients aren't at their best in the winter. This recipe, devised by Westin Kierland chef de cuisine Bryan Williams, makes use of ingredients in good supply during the winter. It is best when the ingredients are cut uniformly to the size of matchsticks.

SLAW
1 large celery root, peeled, sliced thin, and chopped
3 Granny Smith apples, cored, sliced paper thin, and chopped
1½ carrots, peeled, sliced thin, and chopped
1 tablespoon celery seed
Salt, pepper, and sugar to taste

TARRAGON VINAIGRETTE
2 tablespoons finely chopped fresh tarragon
½ cup Chardonnay vinegar or other white-wine vinegar
2–4 tablespoons sugar, depending on the sweetness of the vinegar and to taste
½ cup light vegetable oil
Salt and pepper to taste

FOR THE SLAW, blanch the celery root in salted hot water until tender, about 3 minutes, then immediately transfer to an ice bath to stop the cooking. Combine blanched celery root with the remaining slaw ingredients, taste, and adjust the seasoning.

FOR THE TARRAGON VINAIGRETTE, combine tarragon, vinegar, and sugar. Slowly whisk in oil and then adjust the seasoning.

ADD TARRAGON VINAIGRETTE to the slaw and mix well. Serve chilled.

guadalupe salad with avocado dressing

VELVET ELVIS PIZZA COMPANY, PATAGONIA, ARIZONA

MAKES 4 LARGE MAIN SERVINGS OR 8 SIDE SERVINGS

A restaurant that features both Elvis and the Virgin of Guadalupe in the same setting certainly deserves the term "eclectic." Located in the little southeastern Arizona town of Patagonia, the Velvet Elvis opened in 1998 on December 12, the feast day of Our Lady of Guadalupe, so she decorates one of the restaurant's walls. In contrast, one of the long-standing offerings in gift shops across the border in nearby Nogales, Sonora, Mexico, has been paintings on black velvet. In honor of this regional art form, a black-velvet painting of Elvis hangs over the bar. The restaurant serves mainly designer pizzas and calzones, but there are salads and soups as well. Chef-owner Cecila San Miguel says, "Our Lady of Guadalupe continues to bless the Velvet Elvis, and the Guadalupe Salad is our most popular." This recipe makes large meal-size salads. For side salads, scale all ingredients down. You will have more Avocado Dressing than you need. Refrigerate and use as a topping for chicken or fish or other salads; covered tightly, it will keep for up to two days.

1 cup oil-packed sun-dried tomatoes

12 cups spinach, rinsed and patted dry

1 cup grated Asiago cheese

16 thinly sliced red onion rings

4 large Roma tomatoes, sliced

AVOCADO DRESSING

1 avocado

¼ cup chopped green onion

¼ cup chopped cilantro

1½ tablespoons lime juice

2 tablespoons olive oil

2 tablespoons water

½ teaspoon crushed fresh garlic

Pinch of dried thyme

¼ teaspoon salt

Pinch of dried oregano

½ fresh jalapeño chile, seeded and finely chopped

FOR THE SALAD, put sun-dried tomatoes in a small bowl, and add just enough boiling water to cover. When soft, slice the tomatoes into ribbons and set aside.

FOR THE AVOCADO DRESSING, combine all dressing ingredients in a food processor or blender. Process to achieve medium consistency of heavy cream, adding more water if necessary.

TO SERVE, toss ½ cup Avocado Dressing with the spinach. Divide among 4 bowls. Top each bowl with ¼ cup grated Asiago cheese, ¼ cup sun-dried tomatoes, 4 onion rings, and a sliced Roma tomato.

baby red oak and watermelon salad with orange vinaigrette

THE GOLD ROOM AT WESTWARD LOOK RESORT, TUCSON, ARIZONA

MAKES 4 SERVINGS

This whimsical salad makes delicious use of what are typically considered desert ingredients. Native Americans in the Southwest have been growing refreshing melons for centuries. While oranges are a more recent introduction, they have perfectly adapted to the arid southern regions. Citrus trees of many varieties dot the grounds of historic Westward Look Resort, and the chefs frequently use the fruit in salads, desserts, and drinks. When arranging this salad, stick the base of the lettuce leaves into the watermelon so the lettuce produces a topknot or spray coming out of the melon.

ORANGE VINAIGRETTE

2 cups orange juice
2½ teaspoons roughly chopped shallots (about 2 medium)
¼ cup light corn syrup
½ cup white balsamic vinegar
1 teaspoon sugar
¼ teaspoon lemon juice
¼ cup olive oil

SALAD

4 blocks of watermelon (each about 3 x 3 x 1¾ inches, or 6 ounces), cut from the center
4 ounces Red Oak lettuce
3 oranges, peeled and segmented (or 11-ounce can Mandarin orange segments)
2 ounces micro mizuna sprouts (or mix of broccoli, alfalfa, or radish sprouts)
3 ounces fresh horseradish
4 edible flowers for garnish

FOR THE ORANGE VINAIGRETTE, bring the orange juice to a slow boil in a nonreactive saucepan over medium-low heat and reduce to ½ cup, about 20–30 minutes. Set aside and let cool.

IN A SEPARATE POT combine the shallots, corn syrup, and vinegar. Again bring to a slow boil and reduce by half, about 10 minutes; set aside and cool. Pour both reductions into a blender with the sugar, lemon juice, and olive oil. Mix on high. Pour through a fine mesh strainer and store in the refrigerator. Chill well.

FOR THE SALAD, place 1 slice of watermelon on each plate. Using your finger or a butter knife, punch a ½-inch hole in the top center of each slice; stick equal bunches of Red Oak lettuce leaves in each (see recipe introduction). Divide the orange slices along the front of each plate. Drizzle vinaigrette around the watermelon and orange slices. Place a small bundle of micro mizuna near the base of each watermelon block. Grate fresh horseradish over the lettuce sprays. Garnish with an edible flower.

cocina salad with lime-cilantro dressing

LA COCINA DE LUZ, TELLURIDE, COLORADO
MAKES 4–6 SERVINGS

Many believe the ever-popular La Cocina de Luz (meaning "The Kitchen of Light") serves the best Mexican food in Telluride. Owner Lucas Price makes an effort to buy organic ingredients and looks for foods that have been grown within a hundred-mile radius of the town. If you use a red onion to make this dressing, it will have a reddish tinge, while a white onion will let the cilantro flakes show. This dressing turns even an ordinary salad into something special.

LIME-CILANTRO DRESSING
¼ teaspoon minced jalapeño chile
3 tablespoons minced red or white onion
¼ cup fresh-squeezed lime juice
½ cup canola oil
2–3 tablespoons white sugar
½ teaspoon salt
¼ cup cilantro leaves

SALAD
6 cups spring-mix field greens
½ cup matchstick-size pieces of carrots
½ cup matchstick-size pieces of jicama
½ red bell pepper, julienned
6 tablespoons organic feta cheese, crumbled

FOR THE DRESSING, combine all ingredients except cilantro in a blender and process till creamy. Taste and correct the salt/sugar/lime relationship to your taste if necessary. Add cilantro leaves and pulse until the cilantro is in small flakes and evenly distributed. Do not overblend or you lose contrast. Serve within 24 hours.

FOR THE SALAD, toss the greens with carrots and jicama. Add Lime Cilantro Dressing to taste. Divide into bowls and top with red pepper strips and a sprinkle of crumbled feta cheese.

PRICKLY PEAR FRUIT

The prickly pear cactus is native to the Americas, from Chile to Canada. Columbus took the plant back to Europe at the end of the fifteenth century, and from there it has spread all over the planet. Because the prickly pear produces an abundance of sweet succulent fruits in hot dry climates that aren't very hospitable to other fruits, it has gained great popularity in arid parts of the world.

The fruits appear in the summer through the fall and are about the size and shape of a hen's egg. The flavor of prickly pear fruit depends on the variety, ranging from a light watermelon or honeydew taste, to berry-like, to a bit like cucumbers. The deep garnet-colored syrup known to many as a popular ingredient for Prickly Pear Margaritas comes from the Engelmann variety of prickly pear or its close relatives. Engelmann prickly pears grow wild over thousands of acres of Southwestern desert. Other varieties, such as the tall tree cactus called *Opuntia ficus-indica,* produce yellowish-pink fruits preferred by many people in other countries.

Prickly pear fruit has been a folk medicine—as well as a popular food—in Mexico for generations. Now new medical research has confirmed that prickly pear fruit or unsweetened juice prepared from the fruit helps control diabetes, cholesterol, and high blood pressure.

If you have access to prickly pears, it is easy to make your own juice or syrup. Pick the pears with tongs, clean them, simmer them briefly, then whirl in a blender and strain out the seeds. Add sugar or sweetener to taste, simmer, and you have syrup for interesting drinks such as Prickly Pear Lemonade (page 243) and the Prickly Pear Drop (page 243), baked goods (Prickly Pear–Date Sticky Buns, page 35), Roasted Achiote Pork Loin with Prickly Pear Glaze (page 148), and a dessert called Prickly Pear "Martini" (page 224).

main dishes

Autumn Chicken

SOUS CHEF, TUCSON, ARIZONA
MAKES 8 SERVINGS

Sue Scheff, owner of Sous Chef catering, is known for her innovative, Southwestern-inspired food. Here, she uses pomegranate juice and grenadine, a syrup made from pomegranate juice and sugar. Although pomegranates are not a big commercial crop, many residents of the warmer areas in the Southwest have access to the fruit from trees growing in their yards. Pomegranates are in season in the fall, hence the title "Autumn Chicken." This is an excellent party dish: easy to assemble ahead and slip into the oven at the last minute, elegant and unusual enough to attract compliments, yet not so strange as to turn off the unadventurous. Pomegranates have been hailed as full of healthful antioxidants. If your grocery store doesn't carry pomegranate juice, look for it in any health food store.

5 tablespoons butter, divided
8 large boneless chicken breasts
1½ teaspoons minced garlic
2 tablespoons flour
2 cups chicken broth
¼ cup pomegranate juice
1 tablespoon lime juice
1 tablespoon sugar
1 tablespoon grenadine syrup
1 teaspoon Dijon mustard
2 tablespoons chopped parsley
2 tablespoons chopped cilantro
2 tablespoons Port wine

GARNISH
¼ cup chopped cilantro
½ cup pomegranate seeds

PREHEAT THE OVEN to 350 degrees F. Melt 2 tablespoons of the butter over medium heat in a large sauté or frying pan. Lightly brown the chicken breasts, about 2 minutes each side, then transfer to a large baking dish.

MELT THE REMAINING BUTTER in the same pan. Sauté the garlic until translucent, then add flour and stir until light brown. Add the chicken broth, stirring until smooth. Next add the remaining ingredients and cook a few minutes until blended. Pour over the chicken. Bake for 20–30 minutes. (Make a small slit with a paring knife to see if the meat is done.)

TRANSFER TO A PLATTER and garnish with cilantro and pomegranate seeds.

HUITLACOCHE

In Mexico, they call it *huitlacoche* (wheat-lah-KOH-chay) and consider it a delicacy; in the United States, we call it "corn smut," and farmers try to eradicate it from their fields!

Named *Ustilago maydis* by scientists, huitlacoche is a black fungus that infects sweet corn, swelling a portion of the kernels to an odd shape and turning them black or gray as they fill with spores. The word huitlacoche comes from the Nahuatl language of Mexico, where the fungus has been eaten for centuries, even as far back as the early Aztec and Maya cultures.

Since some Southwest specialty restaurants are now featuring dishes with huitlacoche, farmers are beginning to recognize it as a high-value crop. They have replaced the unappetizing term "corn smut," now calling it "maize mushrooms" or "Mexican truffles."

Still rarely available fresh in the United States, however, huitlacoche is available canned for anyone who wants to try this delicately flavored treat (see Resources, page 249). One 16-ounce can is equal to one pound of fresh huitlacoche, or roughly the amount found on four ears of corn. When huitlacoche is cooked it "melts" and reduces to a sauce. Try this unusual ingredient in Chicken with Huitlacoche and Pineapple Salsa (page 125).

chicken with huitlacoche and pineapple salsa

CIEN AÑOS, ORO VALLEY, ARIZONA
MAKES 8 SERVINGS

Cien Años brings a little bit of sophisticated Mexico City to an Arizona shopping center. Cien Años translates as "one hundred years," and the restaurant's menu genuinely reflects the last one hundred years of the chef's family recipes. Raphael "Paco" Martinez trained as an architect but turned to cooking as a more creative endeavor. It was in his grandmother's Mexico City kitchen that he learned to love many of these dishes. The food at Cien Años has a variety and subtlety not found in more familiar border-style Mexican cooking. Huitlacoche is a fungus that grows on ripening ears of corn (see page 124).

1 pound fresh or canned huitlacoche
½ white onion, chopped
1 clove garlic, minced
1 teaspoon butter
1 large tomato, chopped
1 serrano chile, minced
4 green onions, rinsed and thinly sliced
¼ cup chopped fresh cilantro
8 large boneless chicken breasts

PINEAPPLE SALSA
1 pineapple, peeled
3 tablespoons sugar
2 serrano chiles, minced
Sprinkle of salt
2 tablespoons butter
2–3 tablespoons brown sugar

FOR THE CHICKEN, sauté the huitlacoche, onion, and garlic in butter over medium-high heat until the onion is soft and translucent. Add the tomato, chile, green onions, and cilantro, and continue cooking for another minute or 2.

PREHEAT THE OVEN to 350 degrees F. Using a sharp knife, cut a lengthwise pocket in each chicken breast and stuff with approximately 3–4 tablespoons of the huitlacoche mixture. Close with a sturdy toothpick or thin metal skewer if you wish.

ARRANGE THE CHICKEN BREASTS in a shallow pan. Bake for 20–30 minutes or until done. (Make a small slit with a paring knife to see if the meat is done.)

FOR THE PINEAPPLE SALSA, slice the pineapple into quarters and remove the core, then cut it into 1-inch chunks. Place in a saucepan with water to cover, add the sugar, minced serrano chiles, and salt, and cook over medium heat until tender, about 15 minutes. Drain and leave in saucepan.

IN A 6-INCH FRYING PAN or small heavy-bottomed saucepan, melt 2 tablespoons butter over medium heat, then add brown sugar. Lower heat, stirring constantly, and cook until the mixture begins to form a mass and the butter and sugar are incorporated, about 4 minutes. At this point immediately remove from heat and pour the sauce over the pineapple. Stir to cover the fruit with sauce.

SERVE A PORTION of Pineapple Salsa beside each chicken breast. Rice will round out the meal.

stuffed chicken mole

COYOTE GRILL, SCOTTSDALE, ARIZONA
MAKES 8 SERVINGS

Chicken *mole* (MO-lay) is a traditional dish from Mexico. Its charming origination story explains that some Mexican nuns invented mole out of the only things they had in the kitchen when a high church official was visiting. Traditional recipes often include a long list of as many as twenty-six ingredients. The Mexican state of Oaxaca has the greatest variety of moles, some of which include unsweetened chocolate as an ingredient. This recipe, however, eases the cooking process by using prepared mole paste, available in jars from specialty food stores and some larger supermarkets. The mole sauce may be made in advance and refrigerated until you need it, up to five days.

8 large boneless chicken breasts
3 roasted red bell peppers
8 slices prosciutto
8 slices pepper jack cheese (1-inch by 3-inch)
8 fresh basil leaves

MOLE SAUCE
1½ dried ancho chiles, seeds removed
1½ dried guajillo chiles, seeds removed
6 cups chicken stock, divided
6 garlic cloves, pressed
1½ cups red mole paste (see recipe introduction)
2 bay leaves
Salt to taste
6 cups cooked white rice

FOR THE CHICKEN, preheat the oven to 350 degrees F. Using a small, sharp knife, cut a lengthwise pocket in the chicken breasts. Cut or tear the red pepper into strips. Lay each prosciutto slice flat and layer the pepper jack cheese, basil, and pepper on top. Tightly roll the prosciutto with the layered ingredients inside and place into the chicken breast pocket. Arrange the stuffed breasts in a shallow baking dish and bake for 20–30 minutes or until done. (Make a small slit in the meat with a paring knife to see if it is done.)

FOR THE MOLE SAUCE, while the chicken is cooking, tear the dried chiles into small pieces. Combine 2 cups chicken stock, garlic cloves, and chiles in a saucepan and cook on low heat until the chiles soften, about 10 minutes. Cool slightly, then transfer to a blender and puree. Return the pureed mixture to the saucepan; add the remaining chicken stock, red mole paste, and bay leaves. Stir to combine and cook over low heat, stirring occasionally, until the sauce thickens. Remove bay leaves and salt to taste.

TO SERVE, slice the chicken breasts into 3 or 4 slices each and separate to show the stuffing. Serve with white rice and a generous portion of mole sauce over the rice and chicken.

canyon ranch grilled chicken enchiladas

CANYON RANCH, TUCSON, ARIZONA
MAKES 4 SERVINGS

Guests at Canyon Ranch's health resort learn that healthy eating does not mean deprivation. One of the daily offerings is "Lunch and Learn," during which a chef demonstrates one of the Canyon Ranch recipes, step by step. The Grilled Chicken Enchilada is a favorite of the program. The enchilada sauce is unusual because it is fresh but surprisingly easy to make. The amount of sauce used in this recipe is the equivalent of about one serving of vegetable. If your tomatoes are larger Romas, use fewer, as noted. Try the enchiladas with a garnish of nonfat sour cream.

ENCHILADA SAUCE
1 teaspoon olive oil
12–16 Roma tomatoes, quartered
1 medium onion, sliced
6 cloves garlic
2 teaspoons ground red chile
2 teaspoons ground cumin
½ teaspoon salt
¼ teaspoon pepper

CHICKEN
1 teaspoon paprika
1 teaspoon ground cumin
1 teaspoon ground red chile
1 teaspoon olive oil
2 teaspoons water
4 skinless, boneless chicken breast halves

8 corn tortillas
1½ cups (8 ounces) grated cheddar cheese
½ cup canned diced green chile
Nonfat sour cream for garnish (optional)

FOR THE SAUCE, preheat the oven to 400 degrees F. Lightly coat a baking sheet with olive oil. Place tomatoes, onion, and garlic on the baking sheet. Roast for 20 minutes or until the onion is golden brown. Cool. Transfer the vegetables to a blender along with the ground red chile, cumin, salt, and pepper, and puree until smooth. Set aside.

FOR THE CHICKEN, combine the paprika with the second cumin and ground red chile in a small bowl. Add oil and water and mix to form a paste. Generously pat this spice paste on the chicken breasts. Grill or broil the chicken breasts 3–5 minutes on each side or until juices run clear when pierced with a fork. Cool and slice each breast into 4 long strips.

FOR THE ENCHILADAS, lay the tortillas on a flat surface. Place 2 chicken strips, 1 tablespoon cheese, and 1 tablespoon green chile on each tortilla. Roll and place in a 9 x 13-inch baking pan. Cover with sauce and top with the remaining cheese.

REDUCE OVEN HEAT to 350 degrees F. Cook the enchiladas for 15–20 minutes or until the cheese is melted and sauce is bubbly. Garnish each serving with nonfat sour cream if desired.

chicken with citrus, prickly pear, and chipotle

SOUS CHEF, TUCSON, ARIZONA
MAKES 6 SERVINGS

When you go to a party or event catered by Sous Chef, you know you are in for an interesting meal. This recipe combines all the best Southwest flavors in a smoothly integrated spicy-fruity mélange. Owner Sue Scheff likes to use chicken thighs, as she finds that they have more flavor and are moister than chicken breasts. You can buy the prickly pear syrup (see Resources) or make your own by cooking together prickly pear juice and sugar.

6 large chicken thighs

MARINADE
1 chipotle chile in adobo sauce
1 cup orange juice
2 teaspoons salt

COATING
¼ cup Dijon mustard
¼ cup prickly pear syrup (see recipe introduction)
2 tablespoons chopped fresh cilantro
1 tablespoon whole coriander
1 teaspoon ground cumin

SAUCE
3 tablespoons minced shallots
3 tablespoons butter or oil
1 cup orange juice
1 cup chicken stock
½ cup white wine
1 chipotle chile, seeds removed
6 tablespoons prickly pear syrup (see recipe introduction)
Juice and zest of 1 lime

GARNISH
½ cup chopped cilantro
¼ cup toasted piñon nuts

USING A SMALL, sharp knife, remove skin and bones from the chicken thighs. Arrange the chicken in a nonreactive glass or ceramic baking dish.

FOR THE MARINADE, remove seeds from the chipotle chile and puree until smooth with the remaining marinade ingredients in a blender. Pour the marinade over the chicken, refrigerate, and marinate a minimum of 4 hours or overnight.

PREHEAT THE OVEN to 400 degrees F. For the coating, combine all coating ingredients in a blender. Remove the chicken from the marinade and pat dry (discard marinade). Arrange on a cookie sheet covered with oiled aluminum foil. Brush the tops and bottoms with the coating. Bake for about 30 minutes until nicely browned. (Cut a small slit with a paring knife to see if the meat is done.).

FOR THE SAUCE, while the chicken is baking, sauté the minced shallots in butter or oil over medium-high heat in a medium-size saucepan with a heavy bottom. Add the orange juice, chicken stock, white wine, and the chile, and boil until liquid is reduced to ¾ cup. Transfer to a blender, puree until smooth, and return to the saucepan. Add prickly pear syrup, lime juice, and zest.

TO SERVE, arrange the chicken on a platter, pour the sauce over it, and garnish with cilantro and piñon nuts.

spicy grilled chicken with salad

CHRISTOPHER'S FERMIER BRASSERIE, PHOENIX, ARIZONA
MAKES 4 SERVINGS

For Christopher Gross, chef-owner of Christopher's Fermier Brassiere, cooking is not only a career, it's a passion. He enjoys teaching cooking classes and is active in the broader food community, seeking out the best farmers in the area for his meat and produce. In fact, the name of his restaurant translates to "Farmers' Tavern." Chef Gross also sits on the National Advisory Board for the James Beard Foundation. This chicken is indeed "spicy" and is best served only to those who are ready for a little heat.

MARINADE
1 dry chipotle chile, seeds removed
2 tablespoons olive oil
2 medium tomatoes, seeded and coarsely chopped
2 tablespoons dried basil
2 cloves garlic, minced
1 shallot, minced

4 boneless chicken breasts
4 cups assorted salad greens
2 tablespoons sherry vinegar
3 tablespoons extra-virgin olive oil
Salt and pepper to taste
4 flour tortillas, 8 inches across
½ cup Roquefort cheese
½ cup crème fraîche

FOR THE MARINADE, break up the dry chipotle chile and discard the seeds. Tear into small pieces. Warm the olive oil over medium heat then sauté together all ingredients until flavors are well-combined, 6 minutes, then transfer to a blender and puree.

BRUSH BOTH SIDES of the chicken generously with marinade. Grill the chicken over medium-hot coals 10 minutes on one side, watching to avoid charring. Turn and move away from the hottest coals and grill another 15 minutes, continuing to baste with marinade every few minutes. Do not put any marinade on the last 2 minutes of cooking if you have been dipping the brush in it. Chicken is done when the juices run clear when cut. Remove the chicken from grill and keep warm.

FOR THE SALAD, mix the greens with the sherry vinegar and olive oil and season to taste. Set aside.

TO SERVE, sprinkle each tortilla with 2 tablespoons Roquefort cheese. Heat each tortilla on a grill or in a frying pan until the cheese is soft and beginning to melt. Place cooked chicken breast on one half of tortilla and fold the other half over it. Garnish with crème fraîche. Serve the salad on the side.

tequila and citrus-grilled chicken with mesquite honey

ELEMENTS AT SANCTUARY RESORT, PHOENIX, ARIZONA

MAKES 6 SERVINGS

Nestled in the Sanctuary Resort on the side of Camelback Mountain, Elements offers a menu that changes monthly, featuring whatever is freshest in the local markets. Diners who don't want to gaze at the view of Paradise Valley below can choose, instead, to sit at a communal table and chat with other guests. Executive chef Charles Wiley has a long history in the Phoenix area and in the past has been chosen one of the ten best new chefs by *Food and Wine* magazine. The tequila in this recipe doesn't heavily flavor the chicken, but rather seems to tie the rest of the flavors together. (Read more about Tequila on page 135.)

½ teaspoon whole coriander
¼ teaspoon aniseed
½ cup honey, preferably mesquite
¼ cup fresh lemon juice
1 tablespoon orange zest
¼ cup tequila
3 tablespoons lime juice
2 medium scallions, finely chopped
1 teaspoon finely chopped fresh thyme

1 teaspoon finely chopped fresh rosemary
1 teaspoon finely chopped fresh sage
6 skinless, boneless chicken breast halves (about 5 ounces each)
Kosher salt and fresh-ground pepper

IN A SMALL SKILLET, toast the coriander and aniseed over moderate heat, tossing, until fragrant, about 4 minutes. Transfer to a mortar or spice grinder and grind until you have a smooth powder.

IN A LARGE NONREACTIVE DISH, whisk the honey, lemon juice, orange zest, tequila, lime juice, scallions, thyme, rosemary, sage, and ground spice mixture. Put each chicken breast between 2 pieces of plastic wrap or waxed paper. Using a meat mallet or the side of a sturdy glass, pound each until ½-inch thick. Add the chicken breast halves to the marinade and turn to coat. Let stand at room temperature for 30 minutes.

LIGHT A GRILL or heat a cast-iron skillet, preferably ridged, over moderately high heat. Remove the chicken breasts from the marinade and season with salt and pepper. Grill or sear the chicken, in batches if necessary, about 4 minutes on the first side, or until opaque around the edges. Turn over and cook for about 3 minutes longer, or until opaque throughout. Brush the chicken with the marinade occasionally while grilling, but do not put on any marinade during the last 2 minutes of grilling, as all the marinade must be thoroughly cooked.

TRANSFER THE CHICKEN to a clean platter and serve. Rice and vegetables are good accompaniments.

TEQUILA

· ·

There's something about the taste of a margarita that evokes the feeling of sunny skies, peaceful conviviality, and tropical warmth. Because of our universal quest for that feeling, the United States' consumption of tequila has doubled since 1970—most of that due to the ever-increasing popularity of the margarita. And sales of tequila are still growing by 15 percent a year.

Tequila is distilled from the juice of the blue agave, a tough-leaved grayish green rosette that protects itself with sharp barbs along the leaf edges. The first step in transforming this prickly plant into liquid gold is to hack off the narrow leaves with a machete, leaving a core somewhat larger than a basketball. Since pre-Columbian times, the inhabitants of Mexico have roasted hearts of agave in underground pits and used the juice squeezed from the baked core to make a mildly fermented beverage. Today the production is highly modernized, with the hearts roasted in steam ovens or autoclaves before the sugary juices are extracted and fermented with special yeasts, then distilled. Some varieties are aged in oak barrels and are called *reposados* if they have rested for at least two months, and *añejos* if aged at least twelve months.

Tequila was first imported to the United States around 1870, and in 1893 won the brandy award at the Chicago World's Fair. Today there are about 400 brands of tequila sold in the United States, although some of those don't contain a minimum of 60 percent agave juice, and thus are not considered real tequila. Premium brands advertise on the label that they are made from 100 percent agave juice with no added cane sugar syrup. These tequilas must be bottled at the distillery so that their all-agave composition can be verified.

Actually, tequila is a specialty mescal, much like Scotch from Scotland is a specialty whisky. Tequila originated in the municipality of Tequila, Jalisco, and today only mescal made in the states of Jalisco, Nayarit, Guanajuato, Michoacán, and Tamaulipas may be called tequila. Each legitimate tequila distillery is assigned an NOM (Norma Oficial Mexicana) number. This number is always displayed on the label and is how you can tell if you are buying a legitimate tequila. Any agave-based liquor from somewhere other than these five states or without an NOM is called mescal and, although they are not true tequilas, some of them can be quite good.

Al Lucero, owner of Maria's New Mexican Kitchen in Santa Fe and author of *The Great Margarita Book,* says that tasting and discerning among various tequilas has much in common with wine tasting, and experts talk in terms of flavors of herbs and spices and tannins when comparing brands.

Some tequila aficionados, although not Lucero, believe that it is a waste of good liquor to make margaritas or other mixed drinks with special aged tequilas, as their finer points are obscured by the other ingredients. Instead, they say, these should be sipped straight or neat. You can do your own research while making a Bloody Maria (page 237), a Pueblo Bonito Margarita (page 235), or a Rosalita (page 236).

Tequila is also often used as a marinade ingredient, as in Tequila and Citrus-Grilled Chicken (page 133).

Ana G. Valenzuela-Zapata and Gary Paul Nabhan, in their enlightening book *¡Tequila! A Natural and Cultural History*, cite the old Mexican proverb, "For all things bad, take mescal; for all things good as well." That advice ages well, just like a fine tequila.

walnut-stuffed chicken breasts with wild mushroom demiglace

THE ROSE RESTAURANT, PRESCOTT, ARIZONA

MAKES 8 SERVINGS

Chef Linda Rose established her eponymous restaurant in 1997 in the historic town of Prescott, nestled in the Bradshaw Mountains. During summer rains, the high mountains of the Southwest produce an interesting range of mushrooms, the likes of which enhance this dish. Fortunately, most grocery stores now carry a selection of wild mushrooms, and any variety will do. If you're foraging in the produce department, however, you'll find that a mixture of crimini and shiitake is especially delicious in this recipe.

WILD MUSHROOM DEMIGLACE

1 pound mixed wild mushrooms, thinly sliced (see recipe introduction)

2 tablespoons olive oil

2 tablespoons butter
2 cloves garlic, minced
¼ cup dry sherry
1 cup chicken broth
1 teaspoon cornstarch dissolved in 1 tablespoon water

8 boneless chicken breasts, about 8 ounces each
½ cup finely chopped walnuts
½ cup crumbled Gorgonzola cheese
¼ pound finely shredded prosciutto
2 tablespoons melted butter
Salt and pepper to taste

FOR THE DEMIGLACE, preheat the oven to 375 degrees F. Toss sliced wild mushrooms in olive oil. Spread on a pan and bake 15 minutes, until browned. Set aside and leave oven on while you prepare the chicken for baking.

FOR THE STUFFED CHICKEN, rinse the chicken breasts and pat dry while the mushrooms are baking. With a boning knife, slit a pocket about 4 inches long, along the meaty part of the chicken.

IN A MEDIUM BOWL, mix the walnuts, Gorgonzola cheese, and prosciutto. Divide into 8 portions and place a portion in each chicken breast's pocket.

ARRANGE THE CHICKEN breasts on a baking sheet or dish. Brush each breast with melted butter, then sprinkle with salt and pepper. Bake for 30 minutes.

WHILE THE CHICKEN IS BAKING, finish the demiglace. In a saucepan, melt the 2 tablespoons of butter over medium heat. Add the garlic and sauté until soft but not brown. Add sherry and chicken broth and bring to a soft boil. Add the browned mushrooms, lower heat, and simmer gently for another 15 minutes. Add a little of the cornstarch mixture and cook a few seconds. Add the remainder if needed to thicken for a gravy-like consistency, and then let simmer another minute or 2 to cook all the cornstarch.

TO SERVE, pour the warm sauce either under or over the chicken.

café sonoita tapenade-stuffed grilled steak

CAFÉ SONOITA, SONOITA, ARIZONA
MAKES 4 SERVINGS

Sonoita is a tiny crossroads town in southeastern Arizona in the very heart of cattle country. The café here is a favorite with locals as well as visitors who stop in after a day of birdwatching, hiking, or visiting the local wineries. The Café Sonoita Tapenade recipe makes about three cups, more than you need for this recipe, but proprietors Art and Linda Donatelli advise that you can also serve the delicious blend with sliced meats, crudités, toast points, or crackers. Medallions of filet mignon can be substituted for the New York or rib-eye steak. The recipe calls for three heads of garlic, but you may want to roast five, instead, to be certain there's enough; any extra can be used as a spread or in salad dressing.

CAFÉ SONOITA TAPENADE
3 large heads of garlic
6 teaspoons olive oil
1 cup oil-packed sun-dried tomatoes
½ cup capers
1 cup pitted and coarsely chopped Kalamata olives
1–2 tablespoons olive oil
Juice of 1 lemon
Salt and pepper to taste

4 slices havarti cheese
2 roasted red bell peppers, fresh or jarred, halved
4 New York (12 ounces each) or rib-eye steaks (16 ounces each), ¾–1 inch thick

FOR THE TAPENADE, preheat the oven to 350 degrees F. Cut the top one-fourth from the heads of garlic to expose the cloves, and position each head on a sheet of heavy aluminum foil at least 12 inches square. Pour 2 teaspoons of olive oil over each head, and draw up the foil to make a sealed packet. Put the packet on a baking pan and bake until the garlic is soft and tender, 45–60 minutes. Remove from the oven and cool. Squeeze each clove into a measuring cup. You should have between ⅓ and ½ cup of roasted garlic.

PAT THE SUN-DRIED TOMATOES with paper towels to remove excess oil. Combine the tomatoes and roasted garlic with the remaining Tapenade ingredients in a food processor and whirl for about 45 seconds. If ingredients fling up the sides of the bowl, stop and push them down with a rubber spatula.

FOR THE STUFFED STEAK, spread 1 tablespoon of Tapenade over each slice of cheese and wrap a roasted pepper half around each slice. Using a very sharp paring knife or chef's knife, cut a 3- to 4-inch slit in the side of the steak, working carefully to deepen it to a pocket. Slide a prepared pepper into the pocket. Alternately, butterfly the meat by cutting all the way through but leaving it attached on one long side. Wrap it around the prepared pepper, securing with string or thin metal skewers. (If using filet mignon, grill first, then stack 2 medallions with a layer of red pepper, Tapenade, and havarti for each serving.)

GRILL THE STUFFED STEAKS over medium-hot coals, 7–9 minutes each side for medium-rare, or until done to your preference.

chile–cinnamon rubbed beef medallions

INN OF THE ANASAZI, SANTA FE, NEW MEXICO
MAKES 6 SERVINGS

The Inn of the Anasazi was completed in 1991, but the pueblo-style building looks like it has been around much longer. The interior stone walls are reminiscent of the dwellings of early Anasazi Indians, who inhabited the Southwest region centuries ago. The inn's award-winning restaurant poetically features "foods of the earth from the Native Americans, foods of the soul from northern New Mexico, and foods of substance from the American cowboy." Executive chef Tom Kerpon says this recipe is their signature dish and goes well with White Cheddar–Chipotle Mashed Potatoes (see page 199) or plain mashed potatoes.

CHILE–CINNAMON GRAVY
2–3 tablespoons olive oil
1 medium onion, chopped
1 small carrot, chopped
1 rib celery, chopped
¼ cup chopped garlic
2 teaspoons black pepper
2 teaspoons crushed whole coriander
3 dried red New Mexico chiles, seeds and stem removed, torn into small pieces
1 cinnamon stick
1 lemongrass stalk
½ cup chicken stock
4 cups veal or beef stock
½ cup coarsely chopped cilantro
1 tablespoon dried thyme
1 bay leaf
2 tablespoons cornstarch, dissolved in 1 tablespoon water
Salt to taste
Juice of 1 lime

1 tablespoon cinnamon
1 tablespoon crushed whole coriander
1 tablespoon sugar
1 tablespoon paprika

½ tablespoon cayenne pepper
1 tablespoon salt
4 pounds center-cut beef tenderloin, cut into 12 medallions

FOR THE CHILE-CINNAMON GRAVY, in a heavy-bottomed pot or Dutch oven, warm oil over low heat, then add the onion, carrot, celery, and garlic. Cook slowly to caramelize, adding just enough oil to keep the vegetables from sticking if necessary. When they are very soft and slightly brown, add the black pepper, coriander, chiles, cinnamon, and lemongrass. Sauté for a couple of minutes until the chile pieces are soft, then add the chicken and beef stocks, cilantro, thyme, and bay leaf.

SIMMER UNTIL THE LIQUIDS are reduced by one third, stirring occasionally to prevent sticking. Carefully strain all through a fine sieve and discard the solids. Return the liquid to the pot, add the cornstarch dissolved in water, bring to a boil, then reduce heat and simmer for 3 minutes. Season to taste with salt and lime juice.

SET ASIDE AND KEEP WARM while you cook the steaks.

FOR THE STEAK, combine all dry ingredients in a shallow bowl. Drench the tenderloin medallions in this dry rub as if breading them. Grill over mesquite or chicory coals, 4–9 minutes on a side for medium-rare or to your desired level of doneness.

SERVE 2 MEDALLIONS apiece with the Chile-Cinnamon Gravy on the side.

new york strip steaks with chipotle recado

J-BAR, TUCSON, ARIZONA
MAKES 8 SERVINGS

The name of chef Janos Wilder is synonymous with Southwestern gourmet food. For decades Tucsonans have relished a trip to Janos Restaurant. But for many, the formality and the price found there relegated such visits to "special occasion" status. When the restaurant moved, it became possible for Janos to open an adjacent but less formal venue, and J-Bar was formed. Here diners can enjoy this innovative chef's creations in a casual setting or on the terrace in warm weather. As for this recipe, Janos says, "Essentially, we've taken many of the dry ingredients we use in our mole and turned them into a paste for marinating meat." He also recommends using Santa Cruz Chili & Spice chile powder, his favorite (see Resources). The meat needs to marinate for at least twenty-four hours, so plan accordingly.

MARINADE

2 tablespoons pecan pieces
2 tablespoons pumpkin seeds
1½ teaspoons cinnamon
½ teaspoon ground cumin
1½ teaspoons ground red chile
1½ teaspoons salt
1 ancho chile (seeds and stem removed, torn)
1 chipotle chile in adobo sauce
2 tablespoons raisins
1½ tablespoons orange juice concentrate
6 tablespoons lightly packed brown sugar
1 tablespoon balsamic vinegar
2 tablespoons olive oil

8 New York Strip steaks, 12 ounces each

FOR THE MARINADE, combine the pecans, pumpkin seeds, cinnamon, cumin, ground red chile, salt, and ancho chile in a heavy skillet and toast over low heat for 2–3 minutes. Let cool, then transfer to a food processor or blender, and puree with the chipotle, raisins, orange juice concentrate, brown sugar, and balsamic vinegar.

WHEN THE PUREE IS FAIRLY SMOOTH, with the motor still running, add olive oil in a slow stream to blend and emulsify.

RUB THE MARINADE onto thick New York strips using about 2 tablespoons per steak. Let the steaks marinate 24–48 hours. Grill 8–10 minutes for medium-rare or longer to your desired level of doneness.

santa fe rib-eye steak with tabasco onion straws

ZION LODGE, ZION NATIONAL PARK, SPRINGDALE, UTAH

MAKES 4 SERVINGS

With more than 146,000 acres of cliffs, canyons, and unparalleled beauty, Zion is one of the Southwest's leading attractions for vacationers looking for a memorable outdoor experience. The original lodge was destroyed by fire in 1966, but then rebuilt in only one hundred days. In 1990, the exterior was restored to its original classic appearance. At the lodge's dining room, Red Rock Grill, the chefs serve these steaks with a baked potato and grilled asparagus in season.

4 rib-eye steaks, 10 ounces each
2 cups crumbled blue cheese
2 cups Zion Pico de Gallo (see page 211)

TABASCO ONION STRAWS
2 medium white onions
½ cup Tabasco
¼ cup chopped fresh parsley
2 cups flour
1 tablespoon salt
1 teaspoon pepper
3 cups vegetable oil

FOR THE TABASCO ONION STRAWS, trim off onion ends, then slice into very thin rings, slice each ring in half, and separate. Transfer to a mixing bowl and coat well with

Tabasco. Sprinkle in the parsley. In a separate bowl combine flour, salt, and pepper. Move the onions into this bowl and coat well with the flour mixture.

HEAT OIL to 350 degrees F in a large skillet over medium-high heat. Shake excess flour off the onions before dropping them into the oil a few at a time. Fry until golden brown, and drain on paper towels. Set the cooked onions aside.

GRILL THE STEAKS for 8–10 minutes for medium-rare or longer, until you have reached the desired degree of doneness.

SERVE THE STEAKS covered with blue cheese, Zion Pico de Gallo, and the onion straws.

pink adobe steak dunigan

THE PINK ADOBE, SANTA FE, NEW MEXICO
MAKES 6 SERVINGS

The Pink Adobe is a fixture in Santa Fe, where it has been a local gathering place since 1944. It sits across the street from San Miguel Mission, considered the oldest church in the United States. This dish is a Pink Adobe classic, named after a patron who put green chile on everything. The chefs use mild canned green chiles, so the dish is flavorful rather than searingly hot. To add a little more heat, substitute chopped jalapeño chile for the Tabasco. Note that these servings are very generous; depending on your appetite, you could use smaller steaks.

PINK ADOBE GREEN CHILE
1 medium onion, chopped fine
1 tablespoon olive oil
2 small (4 ounces each) cans green chiles, drained and chopped
¼ teaspoon dried oregano
½ teaspoon minced fresh cilantro
¼ teaspoon salt
1 teaspoon Tabasco

6 New York sirloin steaks, 12 ounces each
Hickory-smoked salt to taste
12 large button mushrooms, sliced thin
4 tablespoons butter
Juice of ½ lemon

TO PREPARE THE PINK ADOBE GREEN CHILE, sauté the onion in oil over medium-high heat until softened. Add the remaining ingredients and continue cooking for 5 minutes. Set aside and keep warm.

FOR THE STEAK, rub hickory salt on both sides of steaks. Broil or grill to desired temperature, 8–10 minutes for medium-rare, turning once, or longer to your desired degree of doneness.

WHILE STEAKS ARE COOKING, sauté mushrooms in butter over medium heat. When the mushrooms are soft, add the lemon juice and cook for 1 minute more.

TO SERVE, transfer the steaks to a platter. Divide the mushrooms over the top of the steaks and smother all with green chile.

pan-seared veal with fresh figs and gorgonzola

ANTHONY'S IN THE CATALINAS, TUCSON, ARIZONA

MAKES 6 SERVINGS

Anthony's in the Catalinas is definitely a special-occasion restaurant. Situated on the slopes of the Santa Catalina Mountains, the restaurant has large windows that look out on the city's lights at night, or lovely fountains and flowers during the day. Consider adding chef Brian Triano's fig sauce to your repertoire, as it can be served with a variety of other meats. Fresh figs are available in the summer, and many people living in the Southwest have them growing in their yards. For more information on figs, see page 147.

2 tablespoons ground dried tarragon

2 tablespoons olive oil

6 veal porterhouse steaks, 12 ounces each

Salt and pepper

6 whole fresh figs, quartered

1 tablespoon minced shallots

¼ cup white wine

⅔ cup spiced rum

½ cup (1 stick) butter, cubed, at room temperature

¾ cup (6 ounces) crumbled Gorgonzola cheese

PREHEAT THE OVEN to 375 degrees F. Mix the ground tarragon and olive oil in a small bowl. Brush the veal with the oil mixture and season with salt and pepper. Heat an oven-safe skillet over medium-high and pan-sear the veal, 30–60 seconds each side. Transfer the entire pan to the oven and roast for 20 minutes. Remove the veal from the pan and allow to rest on a clean cutting board.

RESERVE 6 FIG QUARTERS. Sauté the remaining figs and shallots in veal drippings over medium heat, until the shallots are translucent. Deglaze the pan with white wine and continue cooking until the wine is reduced to a glaze. Add the rum and reduce again, around 5 minutes. Add butter cubes one at a time, whisking evenly into the sauce. Once all the butter has been blended, remove from heat.

TRANSFER VEAL STEAKS to a broiler pan. Divide Gorgonzola among the veal steaks and run under a broiler for about 40 seconds to melt. Serve sauce over veal and garnish each plate with 1 fresh fig quarter.

FIGS

The fig is an Old World fruit that has made itself at home in the Southwest, though it took a long route to find its transplanted home. Fig trees developed in the Middle East before being imported to Spain; from there they traveled with Spanish explorers to the West Indies and later to Mexico, or New Spain, as it was known at the time. The Franciscan missionaries carried figs from Mexico to California. The first fig tree to grow in what is now the United States was planted in 1769 in the garden of the first mission in San Diego. That variety—the same one that does best in the Southwest today—is called Black Mission. Although the vast majority of commercial figs are grown in California, Phoenix has had some small commercial production, and fig trees grow in home gardens throughout the region.

Because they were developed in the arid Middle East, figs can easily accommodate temperatures over 100 degrees F as long as they have adequate irrigation. Figs are excellent eaten fresh with mild cheeses or wrapped in prosciutto as a snack or appetizer. Cooked fresh figs make an excellent sauce for meats. They are used here in Pan-Seared Veal with Fresh Figs and Gongonzola (page 146). When dried, figs can be cut in small bits and used like raisins.

roasted achiote pork loin with prickly pear glaze

THE GOLD ROOM AT WESTWARD LOOK RESORT, TUCSON, ARIZONA ·
MAKES 8 SERVINGS

Many items on the Gold Room menu incorporate Southwestern flavors, including the cactus fruit that grows in the surrounding desert. Just a short stroll across the manicured resort grounds takes you into the lush Sonoran Desert, with its mesquite and palo verde trees and cactus flowers or fruit, depending on the season. Serve this pork loin with Roasted Corn and Sage Mashed Potatoes (see page 203) and vegetables. You can buy achiote paste in Hispanic supermarkets, and rubbing the paste on the roast will take you back to kindergarten finger-painting class! Prickly pear syrup is available in specialty stores and online (see Resources).

2½ pounds pork loin
¼ cup achiote paste (see page 150)
¼ cup olive oil
2 tablespoons kosher salt
Fresh-ground black pepper

PRICKLY PEAR GLAZE
1 jalapeño chile, finely diced
2 cloves garlic, chopped
1 shallot, chopped
1 teaspoon olive oil
8 ounces prickly pear syrup
Juice of 2 limes
1 tablespoon cornstarch
2 tablespoons water
1 tablespoon chopped cilantro

GARNISH
Whole sprigs of cilantro

PREHEAT THE OVEN to 250 degrees F. Clean the pork loin, removing any silver skin and fat cap.

MIX THE ACHIOTE PASTE with olive oil and rub on all sides of the pork loin. Season with salt and pepper. Using a large skillet or griddle, sear the pork over medium-high heat until light brown on all sides. Finish the roast in the oven for about 30 minutes or until the internal temperature reaches 155 degrees F. The meat should rest for 15 minutes after roasting to prevent moisture loss when sliced; cool uncovered for the first 5 minutes, then cover with a tent of aluminum foil for another 10 minutes.

FOR THE PRICKLY PEAR GLAZE, while the pork is cooking, sauté the jalapeño, garlic, and shallot in olive oil over medium heat until softened. Add the prickly pear syrup and lime juice. Bring to a boil and add a slurry of 1 tablespoon cornstarch and 2 tablespoons water; stir well and cook for another 2 minutes. Strain the glaze through a fine mesh strainer, discarding any solids. Add chopped cilantro to the finished glaze just before serving.

TO SERVE, cut pork loin slices about ⅜-inch thick. Fan slices of pork loin on individual plates and drizzle Prickly Pear Glaze on and around the base of the meat. Garnish with fresh cilantro sprigs, and serve with mashed potatoes and a choice of vegetables.

ACHIOTE, OR ANNATTO

MAKES 1 CUP

The small seed called achiote or annatto comes from Mexico, Central America, and the Caribbean, where it is used to give an appealing golden color to foods. The prickly reddish fruits contain up to fifty seeds and grow on bixa trees. The seeds are harvested, cleaned, dried, and sold as coloring. Achiote has begun showing up on menus in the American Southwest, usually as a rub, as a response to the growing influence from Latino cuisines. It has a mild musky flavor and marries well with pork, as in the Roasted Achiote Pork Loin (page 148), and fish, as in the Achiote Salmon Fillet (page 166).

For years, achiote was a hidden ingredient in foods and other products, used to turn such items as margarine, cheese, soap, and cosmetics a bright orange or deep golden color.

You can purchase achiote paste or seeds in Hispanic grocery stores; also see Resources, page 249. If all you can find are the seeds, you can make a simple paste from them with the following recipe:

1 cup vegetable or olive oil
½ cup achiote seeds
Juice of 1 lime
2 tablespoons pineapple juice or orange juice
1 tablespoon dried oregano
1 tablespoon mild ground red chile
¼ teaspoon ground cumin
3 small garlic cloves, minced
½ medium yellow onion
½ teaspoon salt

IN A SMALL SAUCEPAN, heat the oil over medium heat. Add the achiote seeds and cook, stirring constantly, until the oil becomes a rich, orange-red color, about 5 minutes. Remove from the heat and allow to cool.

STRAIN THE ACHIOTE OIL into a food processor or blender, then add the lime juice, pineapple or orange juice, oregano, chile, cumin, garlic, onion, and salt. Process the mixture on high to form a smooth paste. Pour into a glass jar and keep covered in the refrigerator until ready to use. Keeps several weeks refrigerated.

tequila-braised country-style ribs

GRAZE BY JENNIFER JAMES, ALBUQUERQUE, NEW MEXICO
MAKES 6–8 SERVINGS

Graze by Jennifer James is a favorite with Albuquerque diners and consistently appears on local "Best of" lists. These ribs are easy to make, and the tequila, orange juice, and chipotle chile flavors combine with the tomatoes to form a sauce that will linger in your memory (and on your fingers) long after your plate is clean. At Jennifer James, the ribs are served with mashed potatoes.

RIBS
5 pounds country-style pork ribs
½ cup light brown sugar
½ cup 5-spice powder
6 medium cloves garlic, minced

TEQUILA SAUCE
2 tablespoons canola oil
1 yellow onion, julienned
1 tablespoon minced fresh garlic
½ cup tequila
½ cup fresh orange juice.
2 tablespoons chopped chipotle chile in adobo sauce
2 cups canned Roma tomatoes plus juice, chopped
4 cups chicken stock

GARNISH
1 cup chopped roasted peanuts

FOR THE RIBS, clean off any excess fat. Combine sugar, 5-spice powder, and garlic, and rub the mixture well into each rib. Cover tightly and marinate overnight in the refrigerator. The next day, remove the ribs from the refrigerator and let them come to room temperature, 30–45 minutes before cooking.

FOR THE TEQUILA SAUCE, heat oil over medium-low and add the onions; caramelize by cooking slowly until soft and brown. When the onions are almost done, add garlic and stir to blend. Then add the rest of the ingredients and bring to a simmer, cooking 5 minutes. Set aside while preparing ribs for roasting.

PREHEAT THE OVEN to 325 degrees F. Sear each rib until brown in a large skillet over medium-high heat; because of the sugar, the ribs will brown quickly, and you may need to change pans if the browning build-up gets too thick on the pan bottom. Once seared, place all the ribs, side by side, in a deep roasting pan. Add sauce to almost cover.

COVER THE PAN with aluminum foil and cook in the oven 2½ hours, or until fork tender (time will vary depending on the meatiness of the ribs). Remove the ribs from the pan and keep them warm. Transfer the roasting sauce and drippings to a blender and puree, then pour into a saucepan and reheat for serving.

SERVE THE RIBS over mashed potatoes with Tequila Sauce on the side for dipping. Garnish with chopped peanuts.

braised and pulled pork
with orange–honey barbecue sauce

BRITTLEBUSH BAR & GRILL, WESTIN KIERLAND RESORT & SPA, SCOTTSDALE, ARIZONA

MAKES 6 SERVINGS

The Brittlebush Bar & Grill is named after a small Sonoran Desert plant that explodes with brilliant yellow blooms in the spring. The bar is located in the Westin Kierland, a resort and spa that highlights Arizona's history throughout its lush grounds. Brittlebush chef Bryan Williams typically serves this pork as a sandwich on a round polenta roll with a side of Green-Apple–Celery-Root Slaw (see page 115), but the tender pulled meat and roasted vegetables also stand on their own. Since the meat needs to marinate overnight, start this dish the day before you wish to serve it.

1 carrot, diced

2 ribs celery, diced

1 leek, diced

1 onion, diced

½ jalapeño chile, minced

1 Anaheim chile, roasted and peeled (see page 14)

2 tablespoons olive oil, divided

Salt and pepper to taste

1 tablespoon toasted and ground whole coriander

1 tablespoon paprika

2 teaspoons cumin seed, toasted and ground

2 teaspoons ground red chile

1 pork roast (5 pounds)

½ cup chopped cilantro leaves and stems

½ bottle Red Stripe beer, or other light lager

4 cups chicken stock

ORANGE–HONEY BARBECUE SAUCE

½ cup canned Mandarin orange segments

1 tablespoon honey

1 cup ketchup

¾ teaspoon curry powder

¾ teaspoon pepper

¾ teaspoon paprika

¾ teaspoon chopped garlic
½ teaspoon minced jalapeño chile
1½ teaspoons vegetable oil
¾ teaspoon Worcestershire sauce
1 tablespoon soy sauce
½ teaspoon Tabasco
Juice of ½ lemon

PREHEAT THE OVEN to 375 degrees F. Toss the carrot, celery, leek, onion, jalapeño, and Anaheim chile with 1 tablespoon olive oil, season with salt and pepper, and spread out in a 9 x 13-inch baking dish. Roast in the oven 30–45 minutes until golden brown, stirring occasionally. Set aside; cover tightly and refrigerate if holding overnight.

MIX CORIANDER, paprika, cumin, and ground red chile with the second tablespoon of olive oil to make a thick paste. Rub this paste all over the pork roast, cover, and refrigerate for 1 hour. Transfer the roast to a Dutch oven or large casserole dish with a lid. Add cilantro, beer, and chicken stock to the dish, cover, refrigerate, and marinate overnight.

WHEN READY TO COOK, preheat the oven to 275 degrees F. Add the roasted vegetables to the pork dish, re-cover, and slow roast for about 6 hours, or until the pork is brown and pulls easily apart.

MEANWHILE, for the Orange–Honey Barbecue Sauce, combine all ingredients in a blender and blend to a smooth consistency. Store refrigerated in an airtight container, for up to 1 week.

AFTER ROAST IS DONE, let it cool in its dish, then strain off the liquid and vegetables, discarding or saving them for soup. Shred the pork, discarding the fat. Serve drizzled with Orange–Honey Barbecue Sauce or with sauce on the side.

tostadas compuestas

LA POSTA DE MESILLA, MESILLA, NEW MEXICO
MAKES 4 MAIN-DISH SERVINGS OR 8 STARTER SERVINGS

La Posta, one of the best-known restaurants in the Southwest, has a long and colorful history. Originally constructed in the 1840s, it was a stop on the old Butterfield Stagecoach Line and at one time a full-service hotel. This La Posta recipe is made of fried tortilla cups filled with beans and pork in chile sauce, topped with lettuce, tomatoes, and cheese. One of La Posta's most famous dishes, it dates to the 1939 origin of a restaurant on the site and perfects the match between good pork and fine red chile. This also makes an especially colorful dish for a festive occasion.

RED CHILE SAUCE

2–3 dried New Mexico red chile pods
1 garlic clove, minced
¼ teaspoon salt
1 cup water

CHILE CON CARNE

1 pound lean pork
2 tablespoons vegetable oil
1 tablespoon flour
½ cup tomato juice or water
1 teaspoon ground cumin
½ teaspoon oregano
½ teaspoon garlic salt
½ teaspoon salt

TORTILLA CUPS

8 corn tortillas
Vegetable oil for frying

1 cup cooked and seasoned pinto beans
2 cups finely shredded iceberg lettuce
1 cup chopped tomatoes
1 cup shredded longhorn or cotija cheese

FOR THE RED CHILE SAUCE, remove stems and seeds from the chiles. Put into a bowl and cover with hot water until soft, about 20 minutes. Drain the water and tear the chiles into small pieces. Place the chiles, garlic, salt, and 1 cup of water into a blender and puree the mixture until smooth. Add additional water if necessary so that you have a real sauce, not a paste.

FOR THE CHILE CON CARNE, cut the pork into half-inch cubes and sauté in a large frying pan over low heat until brown and moderately dry. Pour off all but 2 tablespoons of any fat that developed. Add flour and coat the pork well. Add 1 cup of the prepared Red Chile Sauce and tomato juice or water; stir in up to ¼ cup more water if the sauce seems too thick. Add cumin, oregano, garlic salt, and salt. Simmer until the pork is completely done, about 10 minutes. If the sauce thickens, continue to add more tomato juice or water, no more than another ¼ cup total.

YOU CAN MAKE THE TORTILLA CUPS while the Chile Con Carne is cooking. You will need a wooden dowel about 2 or 3 inches in diameter and at least 8 inches long; a pint glass jar will also work. Cut approximately 6 1-inch-long slits evenly spaced around the edges of the tortillas.

IN A HEAVY SKILLET, heat oil at least 2 inches deep over medium-high heat until hot but not smoking (about 350 degrees F if you are using a thermometer). Put a tortilla in the oil and push down on the center with the dowel or jar. The boiling oil will force the edges of the tortilla to rise. Fry each tortilla cup until crisp, and drain on paper towels.

WHEN ALL THE TORTILLAS ARE FRIED, reheat separately the Chile con Carne and pinto beans. Put 2 tablespoons of beans in each Tortilla Cup, top with 2 tablespoons of Chile con Carne, then shredded lettuce, chopped tomatoes, and grated cheese. Drizzle with Red Chile Sauce, and serve the remaining sauce on the side.

braised navajo churro lamb

LON'S AT THE HERMOSA, PARADISE VALLEY, ARIZONA
MAKES 4–6 SERVINGS

Lon's is housed in the former home and studio of cowboy artist Lon Megargee. The art on the walls of the sprawling hacienda includes a collection of Megargee's works, traditional Native American rugs and blankets, and other Western memorabilia. The Navajo Churro lamb used in the restaurant is a heritage breed brought to the South-west by Spanish settlers in the sixteenth century, making them America's oldest breed of domesticated sheep. They have been prized by shepherds for their hardiness and adaptability and by the Navajos particularly for their long silky wool, ideal for weaving rugs. Once listed among our endangered species, the Navajo Churro is now making a comeback. You may substitute your favorite root vegetable for the carrots to personalize this satisfying dish.

1 fresh green chile
3 tomatoes, cored and halved
1 medium yellow onion, peeled and quartered
3 tablespoons canola oil, divided
2½ pounds shoulder or leg of lamb, trimmed and cut into 1-inch pieces
Salt and pepper to taste
All-purpose flour for dredging
3 tablespoons tomato paste
4 garlic cloves, minced
2 carrots, peeled and sliced
2 cups wiped and sliced mushrooms
2 cans (12 ounces each) beef broth
2 cans (12 ounces each) chicken broth

RUB THE CHILE, tomatoes, and onion with 1 tablespoon of the canola oil. Place the vegetables directly on a medium-hot grill and cook, turning often, to char the skin of the tomatoes and chile. Just brown the onions lightly and soften. When charred, enclose the chile in a plastic bag and steam for 3–4 minutes. Peel off the tomato skin and cut the tomatoes into small pieces. Remove the stem, skin, and seeds from the pepper. Cut the chile into small cubes. Set all aside.

TO COOK THE LAMB, put 2 tablespoons of oil in a large heavy pot and set over medium-high heat. Sprinkle salt and pepper over the lamb to season and then lightly flour the meat. Brown the lamb pieces in the oil, turning to cook evenly. Add the tomato paste, garlic, carrots, and mushrooms. Cook the vegetables and meat, stirring to prevent browning the vegetables, for about 5 minutes. Add the beef and chicken broths and bring the liquid to a boil.

DECREASE THE HEAT to a slow simmer, cover tightly, and continue cooking for about 1 hour. Add the grilled chile, tomatoes, and onion to the pot, cover, and finish braising the lamb for about another 45 minutes or until the meat yields easily when pierced with a fork.

honey–cilantro rack of lamb

HOUSE OF TRICKS, TEMPE, ARIZONA
MAKES 4 SERVINGS

It might be more fitting to call this place the Houses of Tricks—the restaurant is located in two charming cottages from the turn of the twentieth century when Tempe was a small town and Phoenix was "that other city down the road." Its creative dishes and reasonable prices make it a favorite with locals, including professors and staff from nearby Arizona State University. This recipe sounds odd, but trust these folks—and if you like cilantro, you will love this dish. At the House of Tricks, this is served with Chorizo Potatoes with Ancho Chile–Tomato Sauce (see page 200). The racks of lamb need "Frenching," a technique used to remove fat from the bones of the lamb rack. Ask your butcher to do this for you.

4 racks of lamb, 12–14 ounces each, Frenched (see recipe introduction)
2 tablespoons kosher salt, divided
6 tablespoons ground cumin, divided
3 tablespoons olive oil
1 cup honey
2 bunches fresh cilantro, rough chopped

PREHEAT THE OVEN to 450 degrees F. Season each rack of lamb with ½ tablespoon of kosher salt and 1½ tablespoons of cumin. Heat olive oil in a large skillet over medium-high heat and sear the lamb racks until golden brown on all sides. Place the lamb racks on a baking sheet and roast until the lamb has reached an internal temperature of 120 degrees F for rare or 130 degrees F for medium-rare.

MEANWHILE, pour the honey into a shallow bowl and spread the cilantro on a large plate. Remove the cooked lamb racks from the oven and dip each in the honey, being careful not to get any on the bones. Use a pastry brush to evenly coat and let any excess honey drip off. Then dip each honey-coated rack in the chopped cilantro.

LET THE LAMB REST for 5 minutes after coating and before slicing. If serving with the Chorizo Potatoes, place potatoes in the center of each serving plate and spoon some of the chorizo and sauce on top.

USING A SHARP KNIFE, slice the lamb racks in half between the 2 center bones and place portions on individual plates, leaning against the potatoes or on edge so that the bones are the highest point of the dish. Garnish with a sprig of fresh cilantro.

lamb adobo

LOS SOMBREROS, SCOTTSDALE, ARIZONA
MAKES 4 SERVINGS

This festively decorated Mexican restaurant adds many unusual items—such as this lamb in chile sauce—to the standard fare found in most south-of-the-border eateries. Here you'll find authentic Mexican village flavors prepared by a chef with access to the best ingredients. Slow-cooking meat in chile sauce, like this Lamb Adobo, originated in the days before refrigeration as a way to keep meat from spoiling. This is not a weeknight quick-fix dish, as the shanks need the long simmering to get tender.

12 medium garlic cloves, peeled
4 cups orange juice
6 ancho chiles, stemmed and cleaned
1 stick cinnamon, about 2 inches long
2 teaspoons pepper
2 tablespoons oregano
3 bay leaves
4 whole cloves
2 tablespoons cider vinegar
2 tablespoons brown sugar
2 tablespoons kosher salt
4 tablespoons corn oil
4 lamb shanks, bone in, about 1¼ pounds each
1 cup water

IN A LARGE DRY SKILLET over medium heat, lightly brown the garlic cloves. Remove from pan and combine with all other ingredients, except corn oil, lamb, and water, in a large soup pot and bring to a boil. Simmer 5 minutes or until the chiles have softened. Remove from heat. When cool, transfer mixture to a blender and puree until smooth; strain through a medium sieve to remove seeds. Return the pureed sauce to the pot.

IN A LARGE SAUTÉ PAN coated with corn oil, brown the lamb shanks on all sides over medium heat. Add the browned shanks and water to the pureed sauce and heat to a low simmer. Barely simmer for 1½–2 hours or until the shanks are tender. Watch carefully, and as the sauce reduces, add more water, ½ cup at a time.

SERVE LAMB SHANKS with a side of rice to take advantage of the delicious Adobo Sauce.

cotija rabbit rellenos with charred tomato mole

PRAIRIE STAR CAFÉ, SANTA ANA PUEBLO, NEW MEXICO
MAKES 8 SINGLE-RELLENO SERVINGS

The four-star Prairie Star Café is housed in a renovated 1920s adobe home located near the historic Santa Ana Pueblo. Inside, the dining rooms are roofed with ponderosa pine vigas, while handcarved fireplaces help take the chill off in the evenings. These rellenos are served with a *mole* (pronounced "MO-lay") sauce. The term "mole" comes from an Aztec word meaning "stew." This sauce calls for Ibarra chocolate, a Mexican brand that is a combination of chocolate and sugar; it is packaged in round bars and is usually melted in hot milk then whipped for a frothy hot drink (see Resources). If Ibarra chocolate is unavailable, you may substitute another brand of Mexican chocolate in bars intended for beverages.

RABBIT
6 hindquarters of rabbit, about 8 ounces each, bone in
2 tablespoons dried thyme
2 bay leaves
1 teaspoon black peppercorns
8 cups vegetable stock

CHARRED TOMATO MOLE
5 vine-ripened tomatoes
¼ cup chopped garlic
5 shallots, thinly sliced
2 tablespoons olive oil
2 cups chicken stock
3 small cans tomato juice (6 ounces each, to make 2¼ cups)
2 dried ancho chiles, seeded and washed
2 dried chipotle chiles
1½ ounces Ibarra chocolate (see recipe introduction)
1 tablespoon chopped fresh cilantro
½ cup toasted piñon nuts
1 teaspoon sherry vinegar
1 teaspoon cinnamon
Pinch of whole cloves
Salt to taste

RELLENOS
1 cup crumbled cotija cheese
Kosher salt
Cracked black pepper
8 green Anaheim or poblano chiles, roasted and peeled
2 cups olive oil
3 eggs, beaten
1 cup all-purpose flour

PREHEAT THE OVEN to 300 degrees F. For the rabbit, place the rabbit, thyme, bay leaves, peppercorns, and vegetable stock in a 3- to 5-inch-deep baking pan. Cover the pan in foil and place in oven for 3–3½ hours or until the meat is easily removed from the bone. Remove all meat from bones and chop coarsely; you will need 2 cups of cooked meat. (Broth can be saved for soup and stored in the freezer for up to 2 months.)

FOR THE CHARRED TOMATO MOLE, core the tomatoes and cut in half. Blacken just the skins by putting them over coals on a grill, or under the broiler, or in a dry iron frying pan over high heat. Set aside. Sauté the garlic and shallots in oil over medium heat in a wide saucepan or deep sauté pan until caramelized. Then add the tomatoes and cook until they are softened. Add the remaining ingredients, turn the heat up, and bring to a boil. Then reduce heat and allow to simmer for 10 minutes. Transfer to a blender and puree until smooth, working in batches if necessary. Return to the saucepan and keep warm.

TO MAKE THE RELLENOS, combine the cooked meat and cotija cheese in a medium bowl. Add salt and pepper to taste and set aside.

ONCE YOUR CHILES ARE PEELED, cut a small slit down 1 side of each. Carefully remove seeds. Lightly salt the inside of each chile and fill with ⅛ of the meat and cheese filling, about ⅓ cup.

HEAT OLIVE OIL in a large frying pan to 350 degrees F. Beat the eggs in a wide, shallow bowl. Roll each stuffed chile in flour, then dip in egg to coat. Place the chiles in hot oil and cook until golden brown, turning a few times. Carefully remove them with tongs or a slotted spoon and drain on paper towels.

SERVE THE RELLENOS warm with Charred Tomato Mole and slices of fresh pineapple.

sugar and chile-cured venison chops
with colorado corn sauce

ROARING FORK, SCOTTSDALE, ARIZONA

MAKES 4 SERVINGS

From the cover of *Bon Appétit* magazine to a segment on the *Today Show*, Roaring Fork executive chef Robert McGrath has amply shared his vision of Western cuisine with American cooks. He promotes food that is sophisticated but hearty. Many people in the Southwest region hunt game and thus have access to venison in their own freezers, but there are also excellent sources on the Internet. Chef McGrath serves these chops with Green Chile Macaroni (see page 204).

¼ cup sugar
3 teaspoons dark ground red chile
1 teaspoon kosher salt
4 venison rib chops (7 ounces each)

COLORADO CORN SAUCE
1 tablespoon plus ¼ cup cold unsalted butter, divided and cut into cubes
1 cup sweet corn kernels, fresh or canned
1 teaspoon chopped shallot
½ cup white wine
1 tablespoon plus 4 tablespoons chopped fresh chives, divided

MIX THE SUGAR, ground red chile, and salt together. Evenly rub the mixture over the venison, then cover, refrigerate, and let cure for 6 hours.

WHILE THE MEAT IS CURING, make the Colorado Corn Sauce. Melt 1 tablespoon of butter over low heat. Add the corn kernels and "sweat" them for about 2 minutes, then add the shallots, white wine, and 1 tablespoon of chopped chives. Simmer for 10 minutes, remove from heat and allow to cool, then puree in a blender. As the sauce starts to come together in the blender, add the remaining butter, 1 cube at a time, until all of the butter is used. Strain the sauce and keep warm over very low heat.

AT THE END OF THE CURING TIME, brush any excess dry rub off the venison chops. Grill to the desired temperature over a medium-hot fire, about 3 minutes per side for medium-rare. The sugar in the cure will burn easily so keep an eye on the heat and expect a little blackening.

TO SERVE, spoon corn sauce over 1 portion of the plate and sprinkle with remaining chopped chives. If serving with the Green Chile Macaroni, mound about ½ cup on the other side of the plate, then rest the venison chop up against it.

pastiche salmon cakes

PASTICHE MODERN EATERY, TUCSON, ARIZONA

MAKES 7–8 PATTIES

Chef Don Kishensky suggests pairing these patties with Black Bean Salad (see page 109). They make a wonderful light summer entrée and, should there be any left over, you can serve them on a bed of lettuce for lunch the next day. In fact, they are so delicious this way, you might want to plan for leftovers. Panko flakes are a kind of light, crispy Japanese breadcrumb. They are typically available in any large supermarket, but you can also substitute regular breadcrumbs.

1 small red bell pepper
⅔ cup corn kernels (fresh, canned, or frozen)
3 tablespoons minced garlic, mixed with a few drops olive oil
1 pound salmon fillet
1 beaten egg
2 green onions, finely chopped (about ½ cup)
½–1 teaspoon crushed dried chipotle chile
⅓ cup panko flakes
¼ teaspoon salt
¼ teaspoon white pepper
2–3 tablespoons olive oil

HEAT THE OVEN to 400 degrees F. Halve and clean seeds from the red bell pepper. In a baking pan, place the bell pepper skin side up. Spread corn beside it. Mix the garlic with a few drops of olive oil to reduce sticking, and put it in a small heat-proof dish beside the corn. Roast all for about 30 minutes, stirring garlic and corn occasionally, until lightly browned. If the garlic begins to burn, remove it from the oven. After 30 minutes, the skin on the peppers should be puckered. Transfer them to a plastic bag, seal, and let steam for a few minutes until the skin loosens. Discard skin and chop the pepper.

WHILE THE VEGETABLES ARE ROASTING, remove the skin from the salmon fillet if necessary. In a food processor, pulse the salmon 4 or 5 times. You want a finely chopped consistency, not puree. (You can also chop it with a knife.) In a medium bowl, combine the salmon with the remaining ingredients, except olive oil, as well as the roasted ingredients, and mix well.

HEAT THE OLIVE OIL in a heavy nonstick skillet over medium heat. Using a generous quarter cup each, form the salmon mixture into patties and sauté about 7 minutes per side, until nicely browned.

achiote salmon fillet with yellow pepper vinaigrette and sweet potato–spinach garnish

WINDOWS ON THE GREEN AT THE PHOENICIAN, SCOTTSDALE, ARIZONA
MAKES 4 SERVINGS

Windows on the Green is the five-star Southwestern casual restaurant at The Phoenician. This luxurious resort on the borders of Phoenix and Scottsdale is adjacent to Camelback Mountain. The resort's 250 acres were described by one travel writer as "a bougainvillea-draped Eden." Chef Roberto Sanchez infuses the salmon with a mélange of Southwestern flavors that integrate beautifully. To get the full flavor from the cumin seed, roast it for a minute in a hot frying pan.

MARINADE
2 large ancho chiles, seeds and stems removed
1½ teaspoons annatto seeds (see Resources)
1½ teaspoons chopped garlic
1½ teaspoons chopped fresh cilantro
1½ teaspoons cumin seed (see recipe introduction)
1 tablespoon white wine vinegar
1 cup fresh-squeezed orange juice
Pepper to taste

YELLOW PEPPER VINAIGRETTE
1 large or 2 small yellow bell peppers, roasted, peeled, and seeds removed (see page 14)
¼ teaspoon chopped garlic
2 tablespoons water
1 tablespoon rice wine vinegar
1 tablespoon corn oil
Kosher salt and fresh-ground pepper to taste

SWEET POTATO–SPINACH GARNISH
1 sweet potato, 12–16 ounces, peeled and cut into 12 wedges lengthwise
2 cups fresh spinach
½ cup roasted corn kernels
1 small red bell pepper, diced
1 small red onion, diced
1 jalapeño chile, minced

2 tablespoons cider vinegar
Kosher salt and fresh-ground pepper

4 salmon fillets, 7 ounces each
Salt and pepper
1–2 teaspoons oil
4 sprigs fresh cilantro for garnish

FOR THE MARINADE, combine all ingredients in a blender and puree until smooth. Season with black pepper. Transfer to a bowl and rinse the blender.

FOR THE YELLOW PEPPER VINAIGRETTE, combine bell peppers, garlic, water, and vinegar, and puree in the blender. Slowly add oil in a small stream until emulsified, and season to taste with salt and pepper.

FOR THE SWEET POTATO GARNISH, grill the sweet potatoes slowly over medium coals or on the highest rack under the broiler until tender, about 8–10 minutes. Set aside and keep warm. Warm a medium sauté pan over medium-high heat. When the pan is hot, remove it from the heat and place the spinach, corn, red pepper, red onion, and jalapeño in the pan; drizzle vinegar over all and cover until the spinach is wilted, about 4–5 minutes. Season to taste with salt and pepper and keep warm.

FOR THE SALMON, preheat the oven to 350 degrees F. Season the fillets with salt and pepper, and brush lightly with the marinade. Spray or brush oil on a hot skillet with an ovenproof handle. Place the salmon portions in the pan and sear over medium-high heat until caramelized, about 3 minutes each side. Remove the skillet from heat and place it directly in the oven and cook, 3 minutes for rare salmon or longer to taste.

TO SERVE, crisscross 3 sweet potato wedges in the center of each individual plate. Place a portion of the spinach mixture on top of the sweet potatoes. Brush the salmon again with the marinade and place it on top of the spinach. Spoon bell pepper sauce around the plate, and garnish with a cilantro sprig.

pan-seared salmon tostada with lime sour cream and chile olive oil

EL TOVAR LODGE, SOUTH RIM, GRAND CANYON, ARIZONA

MAKES 4 SERVINGS

The venerable El Tovar Lodge, perched on the South Rim of the Grand Canyon, opened in 1905 and is listed on the National Register of Historic Places. Over the years it has hosted many luminaries, including Theodore Roosevelt and Albert Einstein. Current chef John Nobil has made sure the menu is not stuck in the past, however, by offering innovative versions of Southwestern favorites. At El Tovar, they serve these tostadas with El Tovar Chile-Lime Rice (see page 202) and Fire-Roasted Corn Salsa (see page 209). You can make the Lime Sour Cream and the salsa one day ahead and refrigerate. You can also make the Chile Olive Oil ahead, but store at room temperature—and bring the refrigerated garnishes to room temperature before using them. The sour cream works best when stored and served in a plastic bottle with a squirt top. Although Chef Nobil uses colored corn tortillas, you may not have access to them; plain yellow tortillas taste just as good.

LIME SOUR CREAM
1 cup sour cream

2 tablespoons lime juice

CHILE OLIVE OIL
½ cup olive oil

1½ teaspoons red chile paste (see Resources)

½ teaspoon Tabasco

4 blue corn tortillas and 4 red corn tortillas, or 8 regular corn tortillas

4 salmon fillets, 6 ounces each

2–3 tablespoons canola oil

8 cups spring or mesclun lettuce mix

FOR THE LIME SOUR CREAM, mix ingredients in a bowl with a whisk until combined. Store in the refrigerator; bring to room temperature and shake well before using.

FOR THE CHILE OLIVE OIL, combine all ingredients and mix well. Shake well before using.

FOR THE TORTILLAS, preheat the oven to 350 degrees F. Spread the tortillas on a baking sheet and bake about 8 minutes, until crisp. Remove from the oven and keep warm.

FOR THE SALMON, sear the fillets in a sauté pan in 2 teaspoons canola oil over medium-high heat, about 4 minutes per side for medium-rare. Cook longer if you want it more well done. Set aside and keep warm.

TO SERVE, dress the greens with the Chile Olive Oil in a bowl, using about 3 tablespoons of oil. If serving with Chile-Lime Rice, place a ⅓-cup portion of rice on each plate. Add 2 baked tortillas and spread each with some of the dressed greens.

CUT EACH SALMON FILLET in half, and place 1 piece on each tortilla. Top each piece of salmon with Fire-Roasted Corn Salsa. Carefully pour or squeeze Lime Sour Cream in 2 crisscross lines over the salmon.

blue-corn-crusted rainbow trout

YAVAPAI RESTAURANT, ENCHANTMENT RESORT, SEDONA, ARIZONA
MAKES 4 SERVINGS

The Yavapai Restaurant at Enchantment Resort is named after a small tribe of Native Americans who still live in central Arizona. Executive chef Steven Bernstein serves this dish with Southwestern Succotash (see page 207), baby carrots, and asparagus spears dressed with a little olive oil. The plate is garnished with sprouts or microgreens. You'll have more Lime Beurre Blanc than you need for this recipe, but it makes a delicious sauce for any vegetables and will keep refrigerated for up to a week.

LIME BEURRE BLANC
¼ teaspoon olive oil
2 teaspoons chopped shallots
2 teaspoons chopped button mushrooms
¼ teaspoon chopped garlic
1 bay leaf
¼ teaspoon cracked black pepper
1 cup white wine
1 thyme sprig
1 cup heavy cream
2 tablespoons unsalted butter
½ teaspoon fresh lime juice
½ teaspoon salt
¼ teaspoon white pepper

BLUE-CORN-CRUSTED TROUT
4 rainbow or other trout fillets, 6 ounces each (skin on)
1 teaspoon salt
½ teaspoon white pepper
1 cup blue cornmeal (see Resources)
¼ cup canola oil

FOR THE LIME BUERRE BLANC, add the olive oil, shallots, mushrooms, garlic, bay leaf, and cracked black pepper to a heated saucepan. Cook over medium heat until the vegetables are soft. Add the wine and thyme sprig and continue cooking until the liquids reduce to almost dry. Add cream and simmer slightly, just until bubbly. Whisk in the butter until smooth and incorporated. Remove from heat, strain, and then add lime juice, salt, and white pepper. Set aside. Makes about ¾ cup sauce.

FOR THE BLUE-CORN-CRUSTED TROUT, cut each trout fillet into 3 pieces. Season the fish with salt and pepper. Dip each piece into cornmeal, pressing firmly so it coats the fish well. Heat the canola oil in a large skillet. When hot, add the trout and cook approximately 2 minutes on each side over medium-high heat. Be sure the oil is hot, so that the trout is crispy. Remove the fish from the skillet and let it drain on paper towels; you may have to work in batches. Set aside.

IF SERVING WITH Southwestern Succotash, portion ¾ cup in the center of each plate. Arrange 3 pieces of trout on top, so that the ends meet in the center. Drizzle 2 table-spoons of Lime Beurre Blanc over the fish. Place 2 baby carrots and 2 asparagus spears around the plate. Garnish with sprouts or micro greens. Rice also makes a good accompaniment.

flash-grilled ahi tuna with mango relish and wasabi soy aioli

PASTICHE MODERN EATERY, TUCSON, ARIZONA

MAKES 4 SERVINGS

In this dish originated by chef Don Kishensky, it is important that the sweet potatoes remain a little firm to preserve their flavor and texture. The addition of sweet potato to the mango relish may seem odd at first, but it works well and adds substance. Serve the aioli as a side sauce for dipping the tuna. A green vegetable or salad will make a well-rounded and visually appealing meal.

MANGO RELISH
1 cup medium-diced raw sweet potato
1 cup diced mango
½ cup diced red bell pepper

1 tablespoon chopped chives
1 tablespoon chopped cilantro

DRESSING
½ cup white vinegar
¼ cup sugar
½ cup olive oil
1 tablespoon sesame seeds

WASABI SOY AIOLI
1 egg yolk
Soy sauce to taste
1 cup oil
2 tablespoons wasabi powder or dried horseradish

4 pieces fresh ahi tuna, 6–8 ounces each, about 1 inch thick
Kosher salt and coarsely ground pepper

FOR THE MANGO RELISH, place the diced sweet potato in a medium saucepan, cover with water, and boil until it's no longer starchy but still firm, about 7–9 minutes. Drain. In a medium bowl combine the cooked sweet potato with the mango, bell pepper, chives, and cilantro. Set aside.

FOR DRESSING, combine the vinegar and sugar in a blender and mix well. Very slowly add olive oil until emulsified. Add the sesame seeds and pulse quickly. Add just enough dressing to the Mango Relish to bind the ingredients. Save the remainder of the dressing for another use. Set the Mango Relish aside or cover tightly and refrigerate for up to 1 day. Bring to room temperature before serving.

FOR WASABI AIOLI, place the egg yolk in a blender with the soy sauce and pulse twice. Very slowly add oil until emulsified. Then add the wasabi and pulse 2 more times until combined.

TO FINISH THE DISH, sprinkle the tuna with salt and pepper and grill it with a rack set about 4 inches over a hot fire or broil it on a rack about 2 inches under the broiler. Cook 3–5 minutes on 1 side until brown, then turn and cook to desired doneness. Serve with Mango Relish and Wasabi Soy Aioli on the side.

crayfish–corn risotto

MEDIZONA, SCOTTSDALE, ARIZONA
MAKES 4 MAIN-DISH SERVINGS

Medizona is known for its fusion of Mediterranean and Southwestern flavors. This risotto joins corn with the usual rice base. The tomato adds richness to the flavor without adding calories. If you cannot locate any crayfish tails, use chopped shrimp or lobster. Served with a simple green salad, this makes a lovely, light meal.

6 tablespoons corn oil

1 small onion, diced

4 cloves garlic, minced

1 cup Arborio rice

2 tablespoons tomato paste

1 cup dry sherry

4 cups chicken stock

½ cup corn kernels (fresh, canned, or frozen)

½ cup crayfish tails, peeled (see recipe introduction)

¼ cup grated Parmesan cheese

2 tablespoons unsalted butter

Salt and pepper to taste

HEAT THE CORN OIL in a medium saucepot. Add the onion and garlic and cook over medium heat until soft. Add the rice and cook for about 2 minutes, stirring frequently.

ADD THE TOMATO PASTE and cook another minute, stirring constantly. Add the sherry and simmer until reduced by half, stirring occasionally. While you are doing this, bring the stock to a simmer in a medium pot, then turn down heat and keep warm. Add one third of the stock to the first mixture and simmer until it's mostly absorbed. Add the next third and again cook until it's mostly absorbed by the rice. Add the last of the stock and cook just a few minutes. Stir frequently throughout this process. Add the corn kernels and crayfish tails and continue cooking until the liquid is absorbed and the rice is tender. (If rice is still not fully cooked, add water ¼ cup at a time until the rice is tender.)

REMOVE THE RISOTTO from heat. Stir in Parmesan and butter until melted and incorporated. Season with salt and pepper.

bahian-style shrimp

LON'S AT THE HERMOSA, PARADISE VALLEY, ARIZONA
MAKES 4 SERVINGS

The inspiration for this dish borrows flavors from northern Brazil where *dinde,* or palm oil, is used rather than the annatto oil called for in this recipe. If neither is available, you can substitute corn oil. The chef at Lon's uses fresh shrimp from the Sea of Cortez (also called the Gulf of California) as a special treat when they are available. He prefers the crunchy freshness that is provided by the sweet peppers when added at the last minute, but for ease and more subtle taste, you also can cook the peppers with the garlic and onions. Serve with steamed rice and braised greens.

2 tablespoons annatto oil or corn oil
½ teaspoon minced garlic (about 2 small cloves)
½ cup chopped white onion
1 pinch of crushed red chile, or to taste
2 ounces dark rum
1½–2 pounds large shrimp, peeled and deveined
Sea salt
Pepper
1 cup unsweetened coconut milk
2 tablespoons minced bell peppers (red, green, yellow, or all 3)
1 tablespoon minced chives

PLACE A HEAVY SKILLET over medium heat and preheat the pan for a few minutes. Add the oil, garlic, onion, and red chile. Sweat the garlic and onions, stirring regularly with a wooden spoon and without browning for 2–3 minutes. Add the rum and continue cooking and stirring for 2–3 minutes. Add the shrimp, sprinkle with salt and pepper, and add the coconut milk, then cook the shrimp until it is just opaque, about 4–7 minutes.

TRANSFER THE SHRIMP to a serving platter, leaving the liquid in the pan. Keep the shrimp warm. Return the skillet with the coconut–rum liquid to the stove and over high heat reduce by about one-third. Pour over the shrimp. The sauce should coat the shrimp, and any remaining sauce should pool below the shrimp. Add the bell peppers and chives and give a toss to combine the ingredients just prior to serving.

blackened shrimp with charbroiled tomatillo sauce

MEDIZONA, SCOTTSDALE, ARIZONA

MAKES 4 SERVINGS

When Medizona opened at the turn of the millennium, it was named a Best New Restaurant by the likes of *Esquire, Phoenix* magazine, and several newspapers—and it has only gotten better since then. Medizona chef/owner Konstantin Meshcheryakov offers this dish as an appetizer, but with two recommended side recipes, it is doubtful many home cooks would go to that much fuss. We've increased the number of shrimp per serving to adapt it as an elegant and colorful main dish. Serve with Mango–Olive Salsa (see page 210) and White Bean Hummus (see page 208), both of which you can make in advance, as they hold well.

CHARBROILED TOMATILLO SAUCE
¼ pound tomatillos
1 tablespoon olive oil
½ jalapeño chile, chopped after stem, seeds, and veins are removed
3 green onions, sliced
½ cup chopped cilantro leaves
5 cloves garlic, peeled
¼ cup apple juice
Salt and pepper to taste

SHRIMP
¼ cup ground red chile
2 tablespoons paprika
2 teaspoons ground cumin
2 teaspoons fresh-ground black pepper
2 teaspoons curry powder
2 teaspoons kosher salt
1 teaspoon ground ginger
1 teaspoon cinnamon
1 teaspoon garlic powder
1 teaspoon sugar
¼ cup olive oil

16 extra large shrimp, peeled and deveined
Juice of 1 lemon
2 tablespoons unsalted butter
2 tablespoons chopped cilantro

BEGIN BY MAKING the Tomatillo Sauce. Remove husks from the tomatillos and quarter. Toss the tomatillos in olive oil and grill over medium heat until charred and soft. Alternately, you can place them on a shallow pan and cook under a broiler, or sauté until soft in a hot pan. Let cool slightly. Taste the jalapeño and use an amount to your taste. Puree the tomatillos and all remaining ingredients for the sauce in a blender. Transfer to a small saucepan. Heat just before serving.

FOR THE SHRIMP, mix together all the dry ingredients in a small, shallow bowl. Lightly coat the shrimp in this mixture. Heat the olive oil in a sauté pan. Cook the shrimp in oil over medium-high heat until golden and starting to blacken, then turn them over. Let cook for 1 minute, then squeeze in the lemon juice and add butter, swirling around until the butter melts. Add the cilantro, stir, and remove from heat.

TO SERVE, spread some Charbroiled Tomatillo Sauce on each plate and top with shrimp. If desired, add portions of White Bean Hummus and Mango–Olive Salsa.

soupions à l'ail (garlic calamari)

GHINI'S FRENCH CAFFE, TUCSON, ARIZONA
MAKES 4 SERVINGS

Ghini's French Caffe offers charm, relaxation, and delicious uncomplicated food in the middle of a busy corner shopping center. Chef Coralie Satta-Williams warns that this dish cooks quickly and is time sensitive; it's important to have all your ingredients ready before you begin. At Ghini's, this dish is served with baby mixed greens topped with vinaigrette and a side of basil-grilled baguettes.

1 medium yellow onion, julienned
¼ cup olive oil, divided
¼ cup sweet unsalted butter
¼ cup chopped fresh garlic
⅓ cup dry white wine
¼ teaspoon kosher salt
Dash of cayenne pepper
¼ teaspoon fresh-ground pepper
1½ pounds cleaned and sliced calamari, with tentacles

COOK THE ONIONS in 2 tablespoons of olive oil over medium-high heat until golden and transparent, then set aside.

MELT THE BUTTER and remaining olive oil in a large preheated sauté pan over medium heat. Add the garlic and cook until the garlic starts to smell wonderful and gets a little color. Be careful not to overcook the garlic, as it will taste very bitter.

TURN THE HEAT UP to medium-high. Add the wine and cook until reduced by half. Add cooked onions, salt, pepper, and cayenne pepper; stir. Add the calamari and stir to make sure all pieces get coated with the mixture. Cover and cook for 2 more minutes or until the calamari is tender.

mussels in green chile broth

HILTON OF SANTA FE, SANTA FE, NEW MEXICO

MAKES 4 SERVINGS

The Hilton of Santa Fe occupies a historic estate that belonged to one of Santa Fe's founding families and features architectural elements and artifacts from the 300-year-old home. Guests can dine in a formal dining room that is part of the original house or in the airy enclosed former courtyard. In both cases, visitors get a glimpse of the gracious life of Old Santa Fe. Early Southwestern families were able to enjoy fresh seafood as soon as the railroad arrived in the area, making possible the transport from the coast of shellfish on beds of ice.

¼ cup olive oil

2 teaspoons minced shallots

2 teaspoons minced garlic

2 tablespoons green chile powder (see Resources)

2 pounds black mussels

2 cups dry white wine

2 cups fish stock

8 cherry tomatoes, halved

2 tablespoons chopped fresh thyme or tarragon

Salt to taste

4 sprigs fresh cilantro

HEAT A DEEP-DISH sauté pan over medium heat. Add the olive oil, shallots, garlic, and green chile powder. Sauté for 1 minute. Add the mussels, white wine, fish stock, cherry tomatoes, and thyme. Simmer until the mussels open. Discard any mussels that remain closed. Taste and adjust the seasonings. Divide into 4 large bowls with a garnish of fresh cilantro for each and good bread to mop up the broth.

goat cheese-stuffed poblano chiles with tomato–chipotle sauce

HILTON OF SANTA FE, SANTA FE, NEW MEXICO
MAKES 6 SERVINGS

The Hilton of Santa Fe incorporates part of the historic Casa Ortiz, a short distance from the celebrated Santa Fe Plaza. Casa Ortiz was built in the 1690s by Nicolas Ortiz, who had walked to the region from Mexico City with his wife and six children. In this recipe, mild and flavorful poblano chiles are stuffed with a cheese filling made even richer with piñon nuts and dried cranberries. The cranberries, associated with the boggy East Coast, are a welcome surprise among the other more expected Southwestern ingredients. Serve with black beans and sautéed vegetables.

RELLENO FILLING
½ pound goat cheese
½ pound cream cheese
1–2 teaspoons ground chipotle powder
¼ cup dried cranberries
2 teaspoons chopped fresh mint
2 teaspoons chopped fresh basil
1 teaspoon lemon zest
1 teaspoon lime zest
¼ cup corn kernels (fresh or frozen and thawed)
¼ cup toasted piñon nuts

6 poblano chiles, roasted and peeled (see page 14)

SAUCE
1 teaspoon oil
2 teaspoons minced garlic
1 can (14 ounces) diced tomatoes, with juices
2 teaspoons chopped fresh basil
2 teaspoons chopped fresh mint
2 tablespoons ground chipotle powder
1 teaspoon sherry or vinegar
Salt to taste

3 eggs, separated
½ cup flour
¼ teaspoon salt
½ teaspoon ground New Mexico red chile
2–4 tablespoons dark beer (such as Guinness)

FOR THE RELLENOS, mix all the filling ingredients in a medium bowl. Cover and refrigerate to firm up while you prepare chiles.

MAKE A SMALL INCISION in each chile and open. Carefully remove as many seeds as possible. Divide the chilled cheese mixture into 6 portions and form each portion into 3 balls. Put 3 cheese balls into each chile cavity. Press gently to close. Refrigerate stuffed chiles at least 2 hours.

FOR THE SAUCE, heat oil in a small saucepan over medium-high heat. Add the garlic and lightly sauté for 1 minute. Add tomatoes, basil, mint, chipotle powder, and sherry. Simmer for 5 minutes, season to taste with salt, then transfer to a blender and puree. Keep warm in a non-reactive container.

IN A LARGE BOWL, mix the egg yolks, flour, salt, and ground red chile. Whisk in the beer slowly, since you may need more or less depending on the humidity. You want just enough beer to make a sauce as thick as pancake batter. Beat the egg whites until stiff and fold them into the batter. The batter will hold for several hours if covered and refrigerated.

WHEN READY TO COOK, heat the oil in a deep pan to 375 degrees F. Submerge the stuffed chiles in the batter, then transfer them to the oil with a slotted spoon and fry until golden brown. Remove and drain on paper towels.

SERVE WITH about ¼ cup of sauce per serving on the side.

navajo eggplant with charred tomatillo sauce

ZION LODGE, ZION NATIONAL PARK, SPRINGDALE, UTAH

MAKES 6 SERVINGS

Mormon pioneers in the 1860s gave this area the name "Zion," an ancient Hebrew word that refers to a place of refuge. Its breathtaking scenery includes sandstone cliffs that are among the highest in the world, and the park is home to one of the last free-flowing river systems on the Colorado Plateau. At Zion Lodge, this dish is made up on individual plates. It has been modified so home cooks can make it casserole-style.

1 large eggplant

1 tablespoon salt

10 medium tomatillos

1 cup heavy whipping cream

1½ teaspoons pepper

¾ cup all-purpose flour

3 eggs, beaten

¾ cup bread crumbs

¼ cup vegetable oil, divided

½ cup grated mozzarella

½ cup grated provolone

Zion Pico de Gallo (see page 211)

CUT OFF THE ENDS of the eggplant and discard. Cut the eggplant in half lengthwise, then cut each half into ¼-inch thick slices. Season with salt to draw out moisture. Let it sit uncovered at room temperature until moisture appears, about 30 minutes, and then pat dry with paper towels.

MEANWHILE, peel the husks from the tomatillos, cut the tomatillos in half, and remove the blossom cores. Lightly blacken them on a grill or under a broiler. Watch closely while preparing them. You want the skins blistered and the flesh soft but still juicy. Combine the blackened tomatillos and cream in a blender until smooth. Set aside.

MIX THE PEPPER with the flour. Place the flour, beaten eggs, and bread crumbs each in its own shallow bowl. Dredge the eggplant slices first in flour, then in egg, and then in bread crumbs, laying them in a single layer on a cookie sheet.

FILM A HEAVY FRYING pan with vegetable oil, using just part of the oil. Working with a few eggplant slices at a time, brown on both sides over medium heat, then reduce heat and continue to cook until tender, about 5 minutes total. Repeat with the remaining slices, using more oil if needed. Drain on paper towels.

PREHEAT THE OVEN to 350 degrees F. Alternate layers of eggplant slices and charred tomatillo sauce, ending with sauce, in a 9 x 12-inch ovenproof casserole. Sprinkle with a mixture of grated mozzarella and provolone cheeses. Bake about 20 minutes until the cheese is melted and the sauce is bubbling. Serve with Zion Pico de Gallo on the side.

artichoke ragout

ENCHANTMENT RESORT, SEDONA, ARIZONA

MAKES 4 SERVINGS

Rich and silky, Artichoke Ragout can be made quickly and is delicious served over rice. It can also be used as an elegant side dish, in which case the servings yield would double. Canned truffle pieces and truffle oil are available in some specialty shops; they add an earthy flavor note to this dish, but are not essential. The chefs at Enchantment Resort suggest adding your favorite chopped mushrooms if truffles are not available.

1 tablespoon olive oil
3 cups artichoke bottoms or hearts, diced (canned or frozen and thawed)
½ teaspoon chopped garlic
1½ cups diced tomatoes, seeds removed
1 tablespoon truffle pieces or 2 sliced button mushrooms (see recipe introduction)
1½ cups heavy cream
3 tablespoons chopped fresh parsley
3 teaspoons truffle oil (see recipe introduction)
1½ teaspoons salt
¾ teaspoon white pepper

HEAT OLIVE OIL in a warm sauté pan, then combine the artichokes, garlic, tomatoes, and mushrooms (if you're using them instead of truffles), and sauté over medium heat for about 3 minutes. Add the cream, parsley, and truffle pieces, if using. Continue cooking until the cream is reduced by half, or until the mixture thickens. Finish with truffle oil, if using, and then add salt and pepper.

canyon ranch tamales

CANYON RANCH, TUCSON, ARIZONA

MAKES 6 SERVINGS OF 2 TAMALES EACH

The chefs at Canyon Ranch are dedicated to teaching their guests how to stay healthy while still eating well. While much of traditional Mexican cuisine presents a challenge to those watching their weight or cholesterol, these tamales offer flavor without guilt. They taste remarkably similar to standard green corn tamales, but with a relatively modest calorie count. You'll need about four large ears of corn to produce the four cups of kernels. (Green Corn Tamales are so named because they were formerly made with field corn, picked when it was still tender, before it had matured.) Masa harina is fine corn flour specially milled for tortillas and tamales. If your grocer doesn't carry it, try a health food store or see Resources.

4 cups fresh white corn kernels, cut from cob

1 cup masa harina

1 cup shredded lowfat Monterey Jack cheese, divided

2 tablespoons canola oil

2 teaspoons salt

1 tablespoon sugar

¼ cup lowfat cottage cheese

12 corn husks, soaked in water

2 medium poblano or Anaheim chiles, roasted and sliced (see page 14)

COMBINE THE CORN and masa harina in a food processor and pulse until the corn is finely chopped and the mixture begins to clump together. In a large bowl, combine ¼ cup of shredded cheese, canola oil, salt, sugar, and cottage cheese, and mix gently with a spoon. Add the masa mixture and mix well.

SPREAD ⅓ CUP OF THE MASA mixture on a corn husk, using the back of a spoon. Make a groove down the center of the mixture and arrange 2 tablespoons of chile strips and 1 tablespoon shredded cheese along the groove. Roll the tamales and flatten them slightly. Fold up the pointed tails. Place them in a steamer basket. Steam over medium heat for 30 minutes.

roasted garlic flan with warm pumpkin salsa

MOSAIC, SCOTTSDALE, ARIZONA
MAKES 4 SERVINGS

Deborah Knight, chef/owner of Mosaic, is a consistent winner of the Award of Excellence given annually by *Wine Spectator* magazine. She enjoys developing elegant vegetarian recipes that appeal to *all* of her guests and have the range to complement many wines. This flan is lovely baked and served in ramekins, but if you don't have them, you can bake it in a small casserole dish and scoop to serve. If pumpkin is not available, use winter squash such as butternut or Delicata. Test the spiciness of the jalapeño before deciding how much to add. You can use the oil drained from the garlic to make a delicious salad dressing. A side serving of steamed brown rice or quinoa would nicely round out this entrée.

FLAN
1 cup whole peeled cloves garlic
1 cup canola oil
2 cups heavy cream
¼ teaspoon ground nutmeg
1 sprig of fresh oregano
1 sprig of fresh thyme
Pinch of cayenne pepper
Salt and pepper to taste
4 whole eggs plus 2 egg yolks

PUMPKIN SALSA
⅔ cup small-diced fresh pumpkin (see recipe introduction)
⅓ cup small-diced tart apple, such as Granny Smith
2 red onions, diced small
1½ tablespoons canola oil
½ cup Marsala wine
¼ teaspoon cinnamon
¼ teaspoon ground nutmeg
¼ teaspoon ground red chile
¼ teaspoon ground cumin
¼ cup orange juice
2–3 tablespoons brown sugar

1 tablespoon apple cider vinegar
2 teaspoons minced red jalapeño chile (optional)
1 tablespoon chopped chives
2 tablespoons roasted and salted pumpkin seeds
Salt and white pepper to taste

GARNISH
Long chives
¼ cup roasted pumpkin seeds
Pumpkin oil (optional)

FOR THE FLAN, preheat the oven to 375 degrees F. Place the garlic and oil in a small baking dish, cover, and roast until soft and golden, about 30 minutes. Remove and strain the oil, reserving for other uses. Puree the garlic in a food processor or blender. Cool, then cover and set aside.

IN A SAUCEPAN, infuse the cream with nutmeg and fresh herbs by gently heating over low heat for 15 minutes. Strain and whisk in the garlic puree and cayenne. Return to the stovetop and bring to a boil while whisking. Season to taste, remembering that eggs will be added.

COOL THE GARLIC-CREAM mixture slightly; meanwhile, in a small bowl, whisk together the eggs and yolks. Then carefully add about 1 tablespoon of the warm garlic-cream mixture to the eggs, stirring constantly to temper the eggs. Slowly add the remaining cream, stirring constantly.

PREAHEAT OVEN to 375 degrees F. Pour the egg mixture into 4 ramekins (1 cup each). Arrange in a baking pan and pour water around the ramekins so that it reaches about halfway up their sides. Bake in the water bath until set, about 30 minutes. Remove and let sit for 5 minutes before serving.

FOR THE PUMPKIN SALSA, sauté the pumpkin, apple, and onion in canola oil over medium heat. Deglaze the pan with the Marsala wine after 1 minute. Add the spices, orange juice, and brown sugar, and cook until almost all the liquid has evaporated. Add the apple cider vinegar and reduce slightly. Take it off the heat and fold in the jalapeño (if using), chives, and pumpkin seeds. Add salt and white pepper to taste.

TO SERVE, run a knife along the edges of each ramekin to loosen the flan. Turn out each flan onto the center of a plate and top with warm pumpkin salsa. Decorate each plate with a chive, more pumpkin seeds, and drizzled pumpkin oil if desired.

baked spinach gnocchi verde with alfredo sauce

THE ROSE RESTAURANT, PRESCOTT, ARIZONA
MAKES 4 SERVINGS

Chef and restaurant owner Linda Rose serves eclectic food in a converted early 1900s Victorian home in Prescott's historic downtown. Tables both inside and on the comfortable patio are always graced with single fresh roses. Chef Rose is active in professional restaurant associations and has been honored by her peers for her service to the culinary profession. If you have one vegetarian coming to a dinner party, this can serve as a good entrée while other guests eat it as a side dish. Add small portions of pasta dressed with olive oil or butter. A broiled tomato half or some steamed baby carrots will add color to the plate.

GNOCCHI
1 carton (15 ounces) ricotta cheese
1 pound fresh spinach, chopped
¼ cup butter
¼ cup grated Parmesan cheese
Salt and fresh-ground pepper to taste

ALFREDO SAUCE
2 tablespoons water
2 tablespoons cornstarch
¼ cup brandy
Sprinkle of salt
¼ teaspoon white pepper
1 cup heavy cream
¼ cup freshly grated Parmesan cheese

FOR THE GNOCCHI, put the ricotta cheese into a strainer lined with cheesecloth, and drain off excess liquid.

SAUTÉ THE SPINACH and butter over medium heat, cooking until the spinach wilts. Transfer to a wire strainer and, using the back of a spoon, gently squeeze and strain off excess water. Combine the spinach and ricotta in a medium bowl. Add the Parmesan cheese, salt, and pepper. Fold until blended, then cover and chill the mixture. It will be easier to form the gnocchi when the cheese and spinach are cold.

PREHEAT THE OVEN to 350 degrees F. To form gnocchi, roll the spinach mixture into 16 balls, each a little smaller than a golf ball. Arrange in 4 small ovenproof ceramic dishes or 1 larger baking pan. Bake about 45 minutes or until the balls are firm and lightly browned.

FOR THE ALFREDO SAUCE, combine the water and cornstarch to form a thin paste and set aside. Heat the brandy, salt, and pepper in a saucepan over medium heat. In just a few minutes the alcohol will burn off, then add the cream. Watch closely and stir, as the cream will boil over quickly. When the cream is almost to the boiling point, stir in the cheese. When the cheese has melted, slowly add the cornstarch and water mixture, and cook until it's the thickness of heavy cream. Lower heat, and simmer for a few minutes.

DRIZZLE ALFREDO SAUCE over baked Gnocchi Verde and serve immediately.

stuffed squash blossoms with tomato coulis

MOSAIC, SCOTTSDALE, ARIZONA

MAKES 4 MAIN-DISH SERVINGS OR 8 APPETIZER SERVINGS

Fortunately the days are long past when vegetarians dining out had to content themselves with spaghetti and tomato sauce or a pile of plain steamed vegetables. Chefs such as Mosaic's Deborah Knight relish the challenge of putting together vegetarian meals that are as attractive, tasty, nutritious, and interesting as their other menu items. Quinoa (KEEN-wha) is a grain that comes originally from the Incas, is high in protein and minerals, and is usually sold in supermarkets with the dried rice and pastas. Specialty greengrocers sell squash blossoms, or you can harvest the male squash blossoms from your own garden.

QUINOA STUFFING
½ cup plus 2 tablespoons quinoa
1½ teaspoons olive oil
1¼ cups water
1 medium zucchini, sliced ¼ inch thick
1 medium chayote, sliced ¼ inch thick (substitute more zucchini if chayote is not available)

Salt and white pepper to taste
¼ cup peeled and chopped fresh tomato
1 tablespoon toasted sunflower seeds
¾ cup diced baked tofu (commercial or see following recipe)
2 tablespoons cotija cheese
½ teaspoon chopped fresh oregano
¼ teaspoon chopped fresh or dried epazote (optional, see page 83)
¼ teaspoon chopped fresh rosemary
½ teaspoon cumin seed, toasted and ground
½ teaspoon mulatto or Anaheim chile powder

16 squash blossoms (see recipe introduction)

TOMATO COULIS
4 shallots
2 teaspoons olive oil
6 tablespoons white wine
4 cups chopped tomatoes, peeled and seeds removed, with juices
Dash of lemon juice
Pinch of cayenne pepper
2 teaspoons tamarind concentrate (optional)
2 teaspoons brown sugar
Salt and white pepper to taste

GARNISH
Epazote sprigs
¼ cup toasted sunflower seeds

FOR THE STUFFING, rinse the quinoa in a fine-mesh strainer. Heat olive oil in a medium saucepan and toast the quinoa over medium heat until golden. Add water, cover, and cook over medium-low heat for 12–15 minutes or until tender. Check after 10 minutes; if quinoa becomes dry before it is done, just add a little more water.

MEANWHILE, season the zucchini and chayote slices with salt and pepper. Mark both sides on a hot grill or broil until tender. This will take just a few minutes. Cool and chop them into small dice. In a medium bowl, combine the cooked quinoa, diced zucchini, and chayote with the chopped tomato, sunflower seeds, tofu, cotija cheese, and herbs and spices. Set aside.

TO CLEAN THE SQUASH BLOSSOMS, wipe them gently with a soft wet towel. Carefully open them, and with a small paring knife, cut out the stamens. With a small spoon, stuff each blossom with about 3 tablespoons of the quinoa mixture until 90 percent full. Close by twisting the tips of the flower together. In a steamer, steam the squash blossoms until hot through, about 4 minutes over medium-high heat.

FOR THE TOMATO COULIS, sauté the shallots in olive oil over medium-high heat until translucent. Deglaze the pan with the white wine and simmer until the wine has almost evaporated. Add the tomatoes, lemon juice, cayenne pepper, tamarind, and brown sugar. Simmer 20 minutes. Transfer to a blender and puree smooth, adjusting the seasoning with salt and pepper. Keep warm.

TO ASSEMBLE, place some of the Tomato Coulis in the center of each plate and criss-cross 2–4 squash blossoms on top. Garnish with a fresh epazote sprig and more sunflower seeds.

BAKED TOFU

SLICE 6 SLICES (¼ inch thick) from a block of tofu (about 2½ by 3½ inches). Line a pan with a cloth or paper towel, and lay the slices on the towel. Top with 2 thicknesses of paper towel and a sheet of plastic. Weight with a heavy book. Let the tofu drain for 10–20 minutes. Remove towels. Put a few drops of soy sauce on each slice. Spray oil on a baking pan, and arrange the tofu slices in the pan. Bake at 350 degrees F for 20 minutes.

WINE PAIRING WITH NEW SOUTHWEST FOOD

Only a few decades ago, the only Southwest foods most of us knew were in the taco/enchilada/chile con carne universe. Beer was the obvious choice of beverage—imported Mexican beer, if you wanted to go upscale—cool and refreshing on a hotly spiced tongue.

But today's Southwest chefs are devising sophisticated dishes with complex blends of flavors that can complement or be enhanced by a glass of fine wine. Many restaurants have their own sommeliers, who will offer guidance on a compatible wine once you've decided what to order. But what if you're on your own, with just the wine list and a high-school or college-student server?

Kevin Leeser, a certified sommelier at North Modern Italian Restaurant in Tucson, Arizona, suggests a shiraz as a complement to dishes with roasted corn, believing that the fresh berry flavors of the wine complement the smokiness of the corn. Since Southwestern restaurants now have good access to fresh seafood from the Gulf of Mexico, Sea of Cortez, and Pacific Ocean, Leeser frequently suggests a floral, fragrant white Australian viognier for seafoods to open up any citrus flavors in the sauce.

As for wines originating in the Southwest, Leeser likes wines from the Callaghan Vineyard in Sonoita, saying "they are consistent and only going to get better." To go with spicy food, he suggests a sauvignon blanc or a sparkling wine from Gruet in New Mexico, saying, "The bubbles open up the palate to the taste of the food, and the wine cools down the spiciness."

Chef and cookbook author Fernando Divina of Scottsdale is known for featuring regionally produced food and wines on his menus. He likes the cabernet and merlot from Sutcliffe Vineyards and McElmo Canyon, both in Cortez, Colorado, saying, "Their wines drink well now and complement Southwestern foods famously." He also likes Gruet sparklers for summer dishes.

Ken Colura, sommelier at El Monte Sagrado in Taos, New Mexico, not only takes care of customers at the De La Tierra restaurant but also holds wine seminars for hotel guests. For white wines to pair with Southwestern cuisine, he prefers very crisp and light varieties such as a New Zealand sauvignon blanc or a Macon-Villages chardonnay. For reds, he goes in the opposite direction, preferring bolder wines with lots of fruit, such as a California zinfandel, a malbec from Argentina, or a French syrah.

Most New Mexican wineries have very small productions and don't ship widely, but when he can get it, Colura likes cabernet franc from Casa Rondeña. And like Leeser and Davina, he recommends the sparkling wines from Gruet. "They make seven or eight different ones, and they are all great," he says.

Chef Donna Nordin suggests that both sauvignon blanc and fumé blanc have grassy or herbaceous flavors that seem to pair nicely with assertive spicy foods. She also likes the sweeter whites such as a gewürztraminer, chenin blanc, and Johannesburg Riesling. For reds, she recommends the fruitier, less tannic wines such as a syrah or petit syrah for spicy foods. For those who prefer a lighter red, she likes a merlot or pinot noir.

So that takes care of spicy foods, fish, and corn dishes. But what would be best for the Southwest's more unusual game meats—say the Rattlesnake Empanadas on page 66? Chef Michelle Hansen of the Furnace Creek Inn in Death Valley, California, suggests Kendall Jackson sauvignon blanc. She says, "The dish is a tiny bit spicy and also rich with the buttery texture of the cheese and dough. The smooth fruity taste of the sauvignon blanc works well with no strong lingering aftertaste like a chardonnay."

tortilla lasagna

TERRA COTTA, TUCSON, ARIZONA
MAKES 4 MAIN-DISH SERVINGS OR 8 APPETIZERS

Donna Nordin, the chef/owner of Terra Cotta in Tucson, developed this layered wonder and obviously feels it is reminiscent of lasagna. In the minds of some, however, it could be viewed as an overgrown, supersized quesadilla. Either way, two slices of this dish alongside a big green salad make a satisfying lunch or, on their own, an enjoyable starter.

2 ripe avocados, halved and pitted
4 ounces goat cheese, room temperature
2 ounces cream cheese, room temperature
4 medium cloves garlic, peeled and minced
¼ cup minced mixed fresh herbs (cilantro, parsley, and chives)
Salt and pepper to taste
4 flour tortillas, 10 inches each
2 red bell peppers, roasted and peeled (see page 14)
3 poblano chiles, roasted and peeled (see page 14)

GARNISH
Terra Cotta Salsa Fresca (see page 211)

PEEL EACH AVOCADO HALF, slice thinly, and set aside. Using an electric mixer, food processor, or heavy spoon, mix the goat cheese, cream cheese, garlic, and herbs together until smooth. Add salt and pepper to taste.

TO ASSEMBLE, lay 1 tortilla on a cutting board and spread it with a third of the cheese mixture. Lay the avocado slices evenly over the cheese. Spread a second tortilla with another third of the cheese mixture and place it on top. Lay the roasted red peppers on top of the cheese. Spread a third tortilla with the remaining cheese mixture, place it on top of the red peppers, and arrange the roasted poblanos on top of this third layer. Top the poblanos with the last tortilla. Trim the edges of the stack to make a neater cylinder if necessary.

PREHEAT THE OVEN to 350 degrees F. Cut the "lasagna" into 8 wedges. To cook, heat a nonstick pan or griddle over medium heat with just a few drops of oil. Place a wedge of lasagna in the pan and cook on both sides until golden brown, 3–5 minutes per side. Place all wedges on a cookie sheet and bake until heated through, about 5 minutes. Serve immediately.

sides and salsas

Spiced Artichokes with Backbone Sauce

HELL'S BACKBONE GRILL, BOULDER, UTAH

MAKES 6 SERVINGS

Blake Spalding and Jennifer Castle took on a decided challenge when opening a restaurant in the tiny, remote Mormon town of Boulder, Utah, located in south-central Utah in the middle of the Grand Staircase-Escalante National Monument. The women chef-owners of Hell's Backbone Grill follow Buddhist principles and describe their cooking style as "place-based, regionally relevant food made from scratch." For ingredients such as artichokes, they rely largely on their own organic gardens and orchards and use grass-fed meats raised by local ranchers. Both Blake and Jen previously worked as back-country cooks for expeditions to remote locations, so although opening a gourmet restaurant hours from suppliers was daunting, it was nothing they couldn't handle. (Their book, *With a Measure of Grace: The Story and Recipes of a Small Town Restaurant,* tells their story.) At Hell's Backbone Grill, this dish is served warm, but the chokes can also be chilled, perhaps a preferred serving style for warm evenings.

ARTICHOKES
6 small artichokes

1 lemon, cut into quarters

1 teaspoon whole cloves

10 juniper berries

4 bay leaves

4 stars of anise

1 teaspoon peppercorns

½ teaspoon red chile flakes (more if you like heat)

8 whole medium cloves of garlic

2 teaspoons salt

BACKBONE SAUCE
½ cup sour cream

1 cup mayonnaise

1 or 2 canned chipotle chiles with adobo sauce

2 tablespoons ground cumin

2 cloves roasted garlic

1 red bell pepper, roasted and peeled (see page 14)

Juice of 1 lime
2 tablespoons chopped fresh cilantro

FOR THE ARTICHOKES, trim off stems and use kitchen shears or scissors to cut the spiky points off the outside leaves. Rinse under cold water. Run a cut lemon quarter over the outside of the artichokes (this prevents the cut leaves from turning brown during cooking).

PLACE THE ARTICHOKES in a deep, heavy pot and cover by 1 inch with water. Toss in all the remaining ingredients, then cook over medium heat, partially covered, at a gentle boil until the leaves pull away easily, about 40 minutes.

MEANWHILE, for the Backbone Sauce, in a food processor fitted with a blade, whirl together all the ingredients. Scrape down the sides and continue processing until smooth. Makes about 2 cups; use any extra sauce on meatloaf, burgers, or other sandwiches.

REMOVE THE ARTICHOKES from the water, leaving any bits of spices clinging to them. Serve warm with Backbone Sauce for dipping. It also works to cook the artichokes up to 1 day in advance, store in the fridge, then put them back into boiling water to reheat for 8–10 minutes.

white cheddar–chipotle mashed potatoes

INN OF THE ANASAZI, SANTA FE, NEW MEXICO
MAKES 6–8 SERVINGS

When you are one of America's most honored hotels located in the middle of Santa Fe's historic district, you simply can't serve ordinary mashed potatoes—and this version from the Inn of the Anasazi is anything but ordinary. Should you like your chile flavor on the milder side, consider using fewer chipotle chiles in these rich, creamy potatoes; one may well be enough. It seems silly to fire up the oven to roast just three cloves of garlic, so roast an entire head (or more!) and use as a spread for crackers or freeze for the future. You can also roast a few heads of garlic while baking other foods. Preheat the oven to 350 degrees F. Cut the top one-fourth from the heads of garlic to expose the cloves, and position on a sheet of heavy aluminum foil at least 12 inches square. Put 2 teaspoons of olive oil over each head, and draw up the foil to make a sealed packet. Put the packet on a baking pan and bake until garlic is soft and tender, 45–60 minutes. Remove from oven and cool.

4 baking potatoes, peeled
3 cloves roasted garlic, chopped (see recipe introduction)
1 cup white cheddar cheese, grated
½ cup cream cheese
5 chipotle chiles, crushed, seeds removed (see recipe introduction)
2 teaspoons heavy whipping cream
2 teaspoons butter
Salt and pepper to taste

DICE THE POTATOES and drop into boiling water. Boil until tender, about 15–20 minutes. Drain the water, then transfer the potatoes to a large mixing bowl. Whip the potatoes with remaining ingredients. Season to taste.

chorizo potatoes with ancho chile–tomato sauce

HOUSE OF TRICKS, TEMPE, ARIZONA
MAKES 6–8 SERVINGS

This recipe was developed by Kelly Fletcher, one of the chefs at House of Tricks. Located near Arizona State University in the heart of Old Town Tempe, the restaurant is known for innovative cuisine. In pleasant weather, which is most of the year, diners may sit outside in lush gardens, romantically lit by candles in the evening. If you can't find fingerling potatoes, substitute large red potatoes (a little smaller than a tennis ball) and quarter them.

ANCHO CHILE–TOMATO SAUCE
3 tablespoons olive oil
1 medium yellow onion, peeled and rough-chopped
2 dried ancho chiles, stems and seeds removed
3 medium cloves garlic, peeled and rough-chopped
½ teaspoon ground cumin
2 tablespoons paprika (preferably Hungarian)
2 tablespoons red wine vinegar
2 cans (16 ounces each) stewed tomatoes (or 1 large can, 28 ounces), with juices
1 medium red bell pepper, stems, seeds, and veins removed
1 tablespoon kosher salt

20 fingerling potatoes or 5 large red potatoes, quartered
½ pound chorizo (Mexican pork sausage)

FOR THE SAUCE, heat olive oil in a saucepan on medium-high heat, and add the onion and ancho chiles. Cook until the onions are slightly colored, about 5 minutes. Add garlic and cook for 1 minute longer. Add the ground cumin and paprika and stir for 20 seconds, then add vinegar, tomatoes, and red bell pepper.

REDUCE HEAT TO LOW and simmer, uncovered, for 30 minutes. Remove from heat and puree in a blender until very smooth. Add kosher salt to taste at this time. Pour into a separate container and set aside to cool. This sauce can be made up to 2 days in advance and kept in the refrigerator, tightly covered, before reheating.

WHILE THE SAUCE IS SIMMERING, cook the potatoes. If using large red potatoes, cut them in fourths. Place the potatoes in a pot of salted, boiling water and cook until just tender, about 10–12 minutes. Remove from heat and drain off the liquid. Keep warm.

TO FINISH THE DISH, cook the chorizo for 7–8 minutes in a large skillet on medium heat, breaking it up using a wooden spoon or spatula. Add the ancho chile–tomato sauce to the chorizo and heat until warmed through. Add the potatoes and simmer about 6–8 minutes before serving hot.

corn risotto

TERRA COTTA, TUCSON, ARIZONA

MAKES 6 SERVINGS

Terra Cotta has a reputation for delicious food where pure, distinct flavors take center stage. This rich risotto dish is a celebration of fresh corn. If your main dish is spicy, consider leaving out the jalapeño chiles here and let this be a soothing, milder backdrop.

3 tablespoons unsalted butter
1 small onion, finely chopped
2 cups fresh, tender corn kernels (4–5 ears of corn)
½ cup cream
1 tablespoon minced jalapeño chiles
Salt and pepper to taste
½ cup shredded fontina cheese (2 ounces)
Cilantro for garnish, coarsely chopped
½ cup Terra Cotta Salsa Fresca (see page 211), optional

PREHEAT THE OVEN to 400 degrees F. Melt butter in a skillet over medium-high heat and sauté the onion until lightly browned. Add the corn and cook until hot, stirring often.

POUR IN THE CREAM and bring to a full boil. Cook, stirring vigorously, until most of the liquid is absorbed. Add the jalapeño and season to taste with salt and pepper.

POUR THE CORN mixture into a shallow baking dish. Scatter the shredded cheese over the top. Bake until the cheese is melted and the mixture is bubbling slightly, 5–8 minutes. Serve on warm plates, topped with a little Terra Cotta Salsa Fresca if desired, and garnished with chopped cilantro.

el tovar chile-lime rice

EL TOVAR LODGE, SOUTH RIM, GRAND CANYON, ARIZONA

MAKES 4 SERVINGS

For this side dish, you can cook the rice ahead of time and finish up quickly just before you are ready to serve. At El Tovar Lodge this is served with the Pan-Seared Salmon Tostada (see page 168).

1 tablespoon vegetable oil
½ yellow onion, cut into small dice
½ teaspoon minced garlic
2 tablespoons tomato paste
Juice of 2 limes
3 cups cooked white rice, room temperature
1½ teaspoons ground red chile
1 teaspoon chopped cilantro
Salt and pepper to taste

HEAT A SAUTÉ PAN over medium-high heat. Add oil and sauté the onion until it is translucent. Add the minced garlic and sauté another few minutes, until it is slightly browned.

ADD THE TOMATO PASTE and fry in the pan until it caramelizes and turns lightly brown. Deglaze the tomato paste with the fresh lime juice, then add the cooked rice and stir until the rice is hot. Stir in ground red chile and chopped cilantro.

SEASON to your taste with salt and pepper. Serve warm.

roasted corn and sage mashed potatoes

WESTWARD LOOK RESORT, TUCSON, ARIZONA
MAKES 6–8 SERVINGS

This is an excellent side dish for highly spiced entrées. At Westward Look, they serve it with the Roasted Achiote Pork Loin (see page 148). Recipes like this make having an herb garden very convenient—you can snip off a few leaves of fresh sage rather than having to purchase an entire packet. The number of servings depends on the size of the potatoes.

4 large russet potatoes
Kosher salt
1 cup heavy cream
2 tablespoons (¼ stick) unsalted butter
1 ear fresh sweet corn
4 leaves of broad-leaf sage
Fresh-ground pepper

PEEL AND LARGE-DICE the potatoes. In a medium pot, cover the potatoes with water and a little salt, bring to a boil, and cook until fork tender, about 15–20 minutes. As they cook, heat the heavy cream and butter in a small sauce pot over low heat.

ROAST THE CORN over an open flame from a gas stove or on a barbecue, turning occasionally, until golden and soft. Cut the kernels off the cob. Make a chiffonade of the sage leaves by rolling them like a tiny cigar and then slicing the thinnest ribbons you can with a very sharp knife.

DRAIN THE POTATOES and transfer them to a mixing bowl. Using a mixer, gently mash the potatoes, adding cream–butter mixture, corn, and sage. Season to taste with salt and pepper.

green chile macaroni

ROARING FORK, SCOTTSDALE, ARIZONA
MAKES 4 SERVINGS

If you were like most kids, you loved macaroni and cheese and still turn to it when you need some homey comfort food. Well, this is comfort food with a Southwestern twist—macaroni and cheese with green chile. Chef Robert McGrath considers this a recipe to serve four, but it's so tasty people are sure to want seconds. If you are cooking for four, you may want to double the recipe. The poblanos give plenty of chile flavor with not much heat.

¼ cup diced red bell pepper
½ cup sweet corn kernels
¼ cup diced red onion
2 teaspoons chopped garlic
1 teaspoon corn oil
2 cups cooked macaroni
½–¾ cup puree of roasted, peeled poblano chile (3–4 whole poblanos; see page 14)
⅔ cup grated hot pepper jack cheese
¼ cup heavy cream
Kosher salt and cracked black pepper to taste

SAUTÉ THE PEPPER, corn, red onion, and garlic in oil in a medium heavy saucepan or deep frying pan over medium heat until the vegetables are soft. Add the macaroni, poblano puree, and jack cheese, and stir until the cheese is melted. Fold in heavy cream. Season with salt and pepper to taste.

crispy polenta with gorgonzola sauce

ANDIAMO! ITALIAN TRATTORIA, SANTA FE, NEW MEXICO
MAKES 6–8 SERVINGS

European explorers took the corn they found growing in the Americas back home, and it quickly spread around the world as an essential crop. Andiamo gets its corn and other produce from the farmers market just across the street, a far shorter journey. "Polenta" sounds much more chic than "corn mush," but it is the same thing, just spiced up a little, molded, and cut into charming shapes. This recipe is one of the restaurant's signature dishes, with the polenta cut into triangles.

POLENTA
3½ cups salted water
1 cup non-instant polenta or cornmeal
2 ounces unsalted butter
½ cup grated Parmesan cheese
1–2 teaspoons chopped fresh rosemary
1 tablespoon red wine vinegar
⅛ teaspoon salt
¼ teaspoon cayenne pepper
2 tablespoons olive oil

GORGONZOLA SAUCE
2 cups heavy cream
3–4 ounces Gorgonzola cheese (⅓–½ cup)
Salt
Black pepper
Lemon juice

GARNISH
1 tablespoon chopped parsley
1 tablespoon chopped chives
2 tablespoons bread crumbs

FOR THE POLENTA, bring 3½ cups of salted water to a boil. Slowly add cornmeal in a thin stream, whisking constantly. Cook and stir for 20–25 minutes, until it becomes thick. Add the butter, Parmesan cheese, and chopped rosemary, and stir until well blended. Add the red wine vinegar, salt, and cayenne pepper to taste.

POUR THE POLENTA onto a baking pan and spread to 1-inch thickness. Let it cool, then refrigerate until firm. Cut into 3-inch squares, then slice diagonally into triangles. Cover the bottom of a nonstick sauté pan with a little of the olive oil and heat. Fry the polenta pieces in batches until crispy, adding more oil if necessary. Remove, gently pat dry with a clean dish cloth, and keep warm on a plate while frying the remainder. (Do not attempt to drain on paper towels, or the crispy part will stick and peel off.)

FOR THE GORGONZOLA SAUCE, reduce the heavy cream by about half over medium heat. Whisk in the Gorgonzola cheese until melted and well combined. Season with salt, black pepper, and lemon juice to taste.

POUR WARM GORGONZOLA SAUCE onto individual plates and place polenta on top. Garnish with parsley, chives, and bread crumbs.

southwestern succotash

ENCHANTMENT RESORT, SEDONA, ARIZONA

MAKES 6 SERVINGS (ABOUT 3 CUPS TOTAL)

Enchantment Resort, built in terraces against Sedona's red cliffs, has been named one of the top fifty resorts in the United States. Chefs there give this dish a modern twist, but simpler versions of succotash are as old as the early Native American tribes who farmed in the area a thousand years ago. It contains the three staples of those early farmers: corn, beans, and squash. As a side dish, this succotash complements most spicy Southwestern dishes.

1 tablespoon olive oil
½ cup diced red onion
½ cup fresh corn kernels (may substitute frozen and thawed)
½ cup diced yellow squash
½ cup diced zucchini
1 teaspoon chopped garlic
1 cup cooked black beans (may substitute canned)
¼ cup diced tomatoes
2 teaspoons chopped fresh cilantro
1 teaspoon salt
½ teaspoon white pepper

HEAT OLIVE OIL in a sauté pan over medium heat. Add the red onion, corn, yellow squash, zucchini, and garlic. Sauté until soft. Add the black beans and tomatoes. Cook until heated thoroughly, 5–10 minutes more. Stir in cilantro, salt, and pepper. Serve warm.

white bean hummus

MEDIZONA, SCOTTSDALE, ARIZONA

MAKES 6–8 SERVINGS

When several items on a dinner menu are spicy or highly flavored, as they often are at Medizona, it is nice to have one item that is rich but mild as a backdrop to the more flamboyant flavors. You may use canned beans if you don't have time to prepare dried ones. If your grocer doesn't carry tahini, look for it in a health food store. White Bean Hummus also makes a delicious appetizer when served with toasted pita bread cut into small triangles.

2 cups cooked white beans (see recipe introduction)

¼ cup fresh lemon juice

3 tablespoons tahini (sesame seed paste)

3 small cloves garlic, peeled

1 tablespoon olive oil

Salt and pepper to taste

PUREE ALL INGREDIENTS in a food processor or blender until smooth. If it's too thick, thin with 1 tablespoon apple juice or water.

el tovar fire-roasted corn salsa

EL TOVAR LODGE, SOUTH RIM, GRAND CANYON, ARIZONA

MAKES 4–6 SERVINGS

Corn is still an important staple for the Navajo, Hopi, and Havasupai Indians who live near the Grand Canyon. This refreshing salsa features corn but gets its zip from the minced jalapeño. These little chiles can vary in hotness, so take a small taste and adjust the amount to the level of spiciness you wish. At El Tovar Lodge, they serve this chunky salsa with the Pan-Seared Salmon Tostadas (see page 168). It also makes an excellent, tangy side dish for a hearty barbecue.

2 tablespoons canola oil

3 ears fresh corn

1–2 tablespoons seeded, minced jalapeño chile (see recipe introduction)

¼ large green bell pepper, cut in small dice

¼ large red bell pepper, cut in small dice

1 tablespoon chopped cilantro

¼ red onion, cut in small dice

⅛ teaspoon salt, or to taste

⅛ teaspoon fresh-ground black pepper, or to taste

1 tomato, cut in medium dice

½ cup V-8 Juice, or other tomato-vegetable juice blend

OIL THE CORN and roast over hot coals, turning with tongs, until some of the kernels are lightly browned. You can also do this under the oven broiler. Cool and remove the kernels from the cob with a knife. (Alternately, cut the kernels off the cob and toast them in a heavy, dry frying pan over medium heat until some of the kernels are lightly browned.)

COMBINE THE ROASTED KERNELS with all other ingredients in a small bowl. Hold at room temperature for at least 1 hour before serving, to let the flavors meld. If made ahead, you can refrigerate for a day or 2.

mango–olive salsa

MEDIZONA, SCOTTSDALE, ARIZONA

MAKES 4 SERVINGS

This colorful dish will lift up any plate and wake up any appetite. Medizona, with its Mediterranean-inspired Southwestern cuisine, has been called "a foodie's dream." Toss in a little Nuevo Latino inspiration, and it is dishes like this that have brought chef/owner Konstantin Meshcheryakov his well-deserved reputation for inspired food. Serve with the Blackened Shrimp with Charbroiled Tomatillo Sauce (page 175) or simple grilled fish or chicken.

½ cup small-diced mango
¼ cup pitted, quartered Kalamata olives
¼ cup small-diced tomato
1 tablespoon small-diced red onion
1 tablespoon finely sliced green onion
½ teaspoon finely minced jalapeño chile
1 tablespoon chopped cilantro
1 tablespoon honey
Juice of 1 lemon
Juice of 1 lime
1 teaspoon ground red chile
Salt and pepper to taste

COMBINE ALL INGREDIENTS in a medium bowl and mix well. Chill for at least 1 hour before serving. Can be made ahead and stored for 2 or 3 days. Try leftovers with cottage cheese for lunch.

zion pico de gallo

ZION LODGE, ZION NATIONAL PARK, SPRINGDALE, UTAH

MAKES 2 CUPS

When visiting Zion National Park, it's hard to tear your eyes from the soaring cliffs, but it's also important to look down and enjoy the amazingly diverse ecology. With more than 800 native species, Zion National Park has one of the richest plant systems in Utah. This recipe is salsa for the chile averse—refreshing without being hot. It can be served with chips as an appetizer, or as a salad or relish for fish, chicken, or tacos. At Zion Lodge, it is presented as an accompaniment to the Navajo Eggplant (see page 181).

1½ cups diced tomatoes
½ cup finely chopped white or yellow onion
2–3 tablespoons chopped cilantro, leaves only
2 tablespoons fresh lime juice
Salt and pepper to taste

COMBINE ALL INGREDIENTS in a bowl. Refrigerate for at least 1 hour before serving. Will keep for up to 3 days.

terra cotta salsa fresca

TERRA COTTA, TUCSON, ARIZONA

MAKES 3 CUPS

If you've never made fresh salsa before, you can do no better than taking direction from Donna Nordin, co-owner with her husband, Don Luria, of Terra Cotta. Feel free to adjust the proportions to your taste; regardless, you may never go back to bottled salsa again. Serve as a dip for tortilla chips or as a side dish for chicken or fish or any Mexican dishes.

1½ pounds tomatoes, cored, seeded, and cut into ¼–½-inch dice
¼ cup finely chopped onion
¼ cup chopped cilantro
1 jalapeño or serrano chile, seeds and veins removed, and finely chopped
3 tablespoons fresh lime juice
Salt and pepper to taste

MIX ALL THE INGREDIENTS together and let stand at least 30 minutes before serving. Use within 24 hours.

desserts

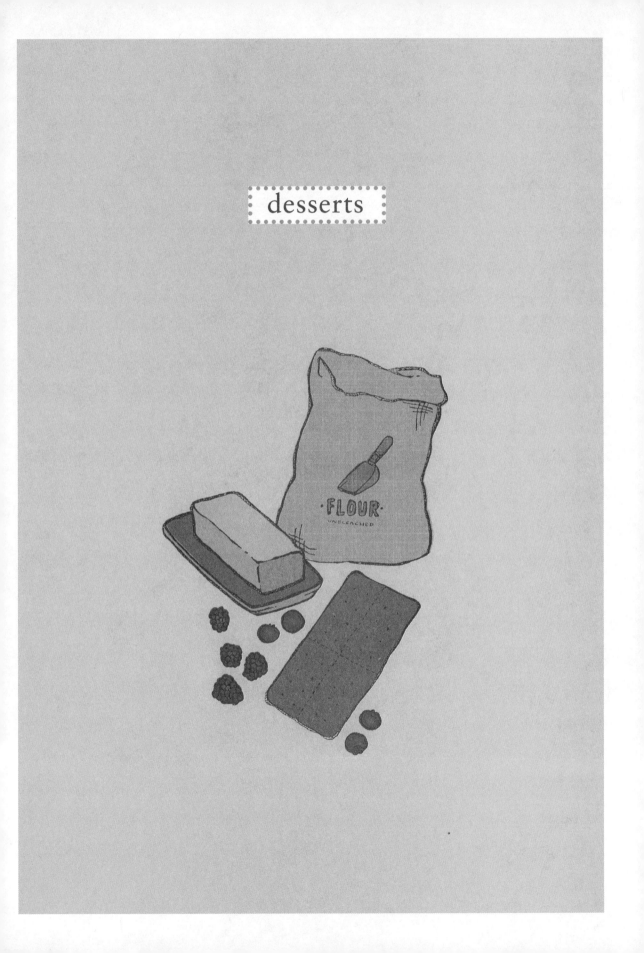

peach, chile, and basil tart

ROARING FORK, SCOTTSDALE, ARIZONA

MAKES 1 9-INCH TART

This unusual tart impresses with its sophisticated flavor. Creative chef Robert McGrath, owner of Roaring Fork, likes to feature seasonal produce, such as peaches, and present Old West recipes with a New West twist. For simplicity, you can also use a prepared uncooked pie crust from your grocer's freezer section.

CRUST
2½ cups sifted all-purpose flour
½ teaspoon kosher salt
½ teaspoon baking powder
⅔ cup cold, unsalted butter cut in cubes
⅓ cup cold milk

FILLING
2 tablespoons unsalted butter
6 cups peeled, pitted, and thinly sliced peaches (about 6 whole peaches)
1 teaspoon minced chile de árbol (see Chile sidebar, page 13)
1 tablespoon lemon zest
2 tablespoons chopped fresh basil
1 cup sugar
¼ cup brown sugar
½ teaspoon ground nutmeg
1 tablespoon cornstarch
8 small scoops vanilla ice cream
8 sprigs fresh mint or basil

PREHEAT THE OVEN to 375 degrees F. For the crust, sift flour, salt, and baking powder together into the bowl of a food processor. Add butter, and process until the butter is in very small pieces. Add milk very slowly and pulse, until the dough becomes smooth and firm. Do not over-process, however, or it will become tough.

ALLOW THE DOUGH TO REST for 30 minutes, then roll out to ⅛ inch in thickness and 2 inches larger than the diameter of your 9-inch pie pan. Lightly flour the inside of the pan and very carefully lay the dough inside, pressing down gently so it doesn't tear. Make sure that the dough tucks into the bottom edge of the pan.

FOR THE FILLING, heat the butter in a heavy pan over medium-high heat and sauté the peaches, chile de árbol, lemon zest, and fresh basil until just tender. Add sugar, brown sugar, nutmeg, and cornstarch to the peaches, mix together, and remove from heat.

POUR THE PEACHES into the dough-lined pie pan and bake for 30 minutes. Check the tart, and if it needs more browning on top, lower heat to 325 degrees F and bake for another 10 minutes. Remove from the oven and allow to cool for 10 minutes before serving.

texas millionaire pie

THE DAILY PIE CAFÉ, PIE TOWN, NEW MEXICO
MAKES 1 8-INCH PIE

Pie Town sits on the Continental Divide at an elevation of 8,000 feet, a name and height that together mandate a place with hearty servings of, well, pie. At the Daily Pie Café, Peggy Rawl has adjusted a recipe she found for Texas Millionaire Pie to suit her taste and that of her customers. Make this pie at least an hour before serving so it can set up in the refrigerator. Peggy and her husband, Michael, will also serve you a good lunch—that is, if you think you should have something substantial before dessert.

CHOCOLATE GRAHAM CRUST
½ box chocolate graham crackers
¼ cup sugar
¼ cup (½ stick) butter, melted

FILLING
4 ounces cream cheese, softened
¼ cup sugar
⅔ cup drained canned crushed pineapple
¾ cup coconut flakes
¾ cup broken pecans, plus 6 halves for decoration (optional)
8 ounces Cool Whip, or similar product

FOR THE CRUST, crush the grahams in a food processor. Put them into a bowl and mix in the sugar. Add the melted butter and stir with a fork until blended. Press into an 8-inch pie pan.

FOR THE FILLING, mix the cream cheese, sugar, and pineapple with a mixer until blended. Next, stir in by hand the coconut and broken pecans. Fold in the Cool Whip. Pour the filling into the crust, and top with pecan halves to indicate each of 6 slices. Refrigerate for at least 1 hour before serving.

brown butter berry tart

YAVAPAI RESTAURANT, ENCHANTMENT RESORT, SEDONA, ARIZONA
MAKES 1 8-INCH TART

Guests of the Enchantment Resort who dine in the Yavapai Restaurant are never cut off from the extravagant natural beauty they came to see. The windows in the restaurant provide 180-degree views of the red rock cliffs of Boynton Canyon. Enchantment chefs probably don't go berry-picking, but experienced hikers know where to find stands of wild raspberries and blackberries in the mountainous forests to the north of Sedona. It takes real self-control to carry the berries all the way home without tasting just one—and then another and another. If you don't have access to wild berries, or much self-control, you can buy the berries in a store or local farmers' market.

Uncooked pie dough for 8-inch tart, purchased or homemade

FILLING
2 cups fresh mixed berries, such as raspberries, blueberries, and blackberries
3 eggs
1 cup sugar
½ cup flour
1 teaspoon vanilla extract
½ cup (1 stick) butter

PLACE THE PIE DOUGH in a tart pan and chill. Distribute the berries over the chilled tart shell. Combine the eggs, sugar, and flour in a mixing bowl. Mix well and add vanilla extract. In a saucepan over medium heat, brown the butter to a nutty smell, stirring to get an even brown color. Add to the mixing bowl and mix well with the other ingredients. Pour the filling over the berries. Bake at 350 degrees F for 50–60 minutes, or until lightly brown.

SERVE WARM OR CHILLED with any flavor of fruit puree, sorbet, or whipped cream.

new mexican apple pie

THE DAILY PIE CAFÉ, PIE TOWN, NEW MEXICO
MAKES 1 9-INCH PIE

At a café called Daily Pie, you expect at least some of the pies to be unusual—and all of them to be good. This apple pie fills the bill on both counts. It is frequently said that New Mexicans put chile in everything, and this pie also shows that there's some truth to that saying. The chile combines very well with the apples, and the piñon nuts add further texture. If you find yourself driving west of Soccorro, New Mexico, plan to stop in at the café and check out that day's offerings.

Pastry for double-crust pie, purchased or homemade

FILLING

1 cup piñon nuts
6 cups peeled and thinly sliced Granny Smith apples (about 6–7 whole)
1 tablespoon lemon juice
1 cup sugar
3 tablespoons flour
2 teaspoons cinnamon
½ teaspoon ground nutmeg
⅓ cup green chile, hot or mild, depending on taste

PREHEAT THE OVEN to 425 degrees F. For the crust, if using homemade or unshaped dough, roll out pastry into 2 rounds. Place 1 crust into a 9-inch pan and spread nuts across it, creating 1 layer.

FOR THE FILLING, in a large bowl, combine all the remaining ingredients, then spoon the apple/chile mixture over the nuts and crust. Put the top crust on and gently seal and flute the edge all the way around. Slice 6 vents in the top crust.

BAKE FOR 15 MINUTES. Lower the oven to 400 degrees F and bake for an additional 45 minutes, or until juices are thick and bubbly through the vents. (This is a juicy pie, so to catch any run-over, position a baking sheet on the rack under the pie.) Remove from oven and let set for 10 minutes before serving.

SERVE WARM with vanilla ice cream or thick slices of cheddar cheese.

caramel pecan cheesecake

ROCKING V CAFÉ, KANAB, UTAH

MAKES A 9- OR 10-INCH CHEESECAKE, 12 SERVINGS

Vicky Cooper, who with her husband, Victor, runs the Rocking V Café in Kanab, made this cheesecake for KNBC's program called *The Travel Cafe,* which appears in Los Angeles and San Diego and also aired on the Travel Channel. The cheesecake became so popular that the Rocking V Café now features it three or four times each week. Vicky emphasizes that the delicious flavor calls for real vanilla extract, not an artificial substitute.

CRUST

2 cups crushed graham crackers

½ cup melted butter

½ cup chopped pecans

FILLING

1½ pounds (24 ounces) softened cream cheese

1 cup sugar

3 eggs

½ teaspoon salt

2 tablespoons vanilla extract (see recipe introduction)

¼ cup Amaretto, or other almond-flavored liqueur

3 cups sour cream

1 cup prepared caramel topping

1 cup pecan halves

Whipped cream for garnish

FOR THE CRUST, preheat the oven to 350 degrees F. In a medium bowl, mix the ingredients together and press into the bottom of 9- or 10-inch springform cake pan. Bake 8 minutes. Cool while preparing the filling, and turn the oven down to 325 degrees F.

FOR THE FILLING, in a large bowl, whip the cream cheese until smooth. Beat in the sugar. Add the eggs and beat until smooth. Add salt, vanilla extract, and Amaretto, again beating until smooth. Beat in the sour cream until just blended.

POUR INTO THE CRUST. Gently stir ¾ cup caramel topping into the top half of the cheesecake, being careful not to lift the graham crust into the mixture. Arrange pecan halves around the edges of the pan. Drizzle remaining ¼ cup caramel syrup over the pecan halves.

BAKE FOR 50 MINUTES, then shut off the oven and leave the cheesecake in it for 1 hour. Cool the cheesecake on the countertop for another hour, then refrigerate for 6 hours. Remove the springform ring. Place the cheesecake in the freezer for 30 minutes before serving.

TO SERVE, dip a knife into hot water between each cut, slicing the cheesecake into 12 pieces. Serve with a dollop of whipped cream. Cover unused cheesecake tightly with plastic wrap. Stays fresh up to 3 or 4 days in refrigerator.

the rose chocolate mousse

THE ROSE RESTAURANT, PRESCOTT, ARIZONA

MAKES 10 SERVINGS

Chef Linda Rose is known for her innovative cuisine, served in a serene setting in the historic mountain town of Prescott. "We set out to create a restaurant that offers fine dining with a comfortable atmosphere," she says. "We want our customers to have a complete dining experience, from the moment they make their reservation until they leave the property." This mousse is an ideal representation of that experience, light yet rich and not difficult to make. To avoid overcooking the egg-yolk mixture when combining with the chocolate, first stir just a tablespoon of the hot chocolate mixture into the yolks.

8 egg whites
4 egg yolks
1½ cups (3 sticks) butter
10 ounces semisweet dark chocolate
1½ tablespoons sweet sherry
1½ tablespoons brandy
2 tablespoons plus 2 teaspoons sugar
2 cups heavy cream

SEPARATE THE EGGS, retaining 8 egg whites and 4 yolks; set both aside. Combine the butter and chocolate in a double boiler; when the chocolate is melted, remove from heat and whisk until smooth and blended.

COMBINE EGG YOLKS, sherry, and brandy in a mixing bowl, and beat until creamy. Stir just a little of the chocolate mixture into the yolks to temper them (see recipe introduction). Slowly add the rest of the yolk mixture into the chocolate, beating gently until combined. Let stand at room temperature till cool, about 30 minutes.

WASH MIXER BEATERS with hot soapy water so they are absolutely clean. When the chocolate-yolk mixture has cooled, combine the egg whites and sugar in a bowl, beating until stiff peaks form. In a large bowl, fold together (do not whip) the chocolate and egg whites.

IN ANOTHER LARGE BOWL, whip the heavy cream until stiff. Fold together the chocolate mixture and heavy cream. Refrigerate till chilled, then pipe or spoon into serving glasses or cups.

flourless chocolate cake

HEARTLINE CAFÉ, SEDONA, ARIZONA
MAKES AN 8-INCH CAKE, 10 SERVINGS

The "heartline" in this charming café's name comes from Zuni fetishes on which a line is painted or inlaid that represents the life force, or as it is sometimes explained: health, long life, and good luck. It would be good luck indeed to be eating a piece of this cake on the café's outdoor patio, warmed by the fireplace if there is a chill in the air. At the Heartline, the cake is served with chocolate sauce, but it is rich enough to stand on its own. When separating eggs, first put each white into a cup or saucer before adding to the other whites. That way if you have had a problem with a broken yolk, you will not contaminate all the whites. Even a tiny bit of yolk will prevent the whites from whipping to their full potential.

½ pound bittersweet chocolate
⅓ cup butter, room temperature
1 cup sugar
8 eggs, separated (see recipe introduction)

PREHEAT THE OVEN to 325 degrees F. Grease an 8-inch springform cake pan. Melt the chocolate in a double boiler and then let cool. Using an electric mixer, cream the butter and sugar together at low speed. Set aside.

CLEAN THE BEATERS with soap and hot water to remove all grease. Beat the egg whites on medium until soft peaks form; set aside.

MIX THE COOLED MELTED CHOCOLATE into the egg yolks on low speed until smooth, then add the butter–sugar mixture and continue mixing until smooth. Increase the mixer speed to medium and continue to mix, about 2 more minutes.

GENTLY FOLD IN THE EGG whites, one third at a time.

POUR THE BATTER into the prepared pan and bake 20–30 minutes, until a toothpick comes out barely moist. Remove from oven and cool for 20 minutes before removing from pan. Slice into 10 wedges.

prickly pear "martini" and cornmeal–lime cookie

DE LA TIERRA, EL MONTE SAGRADO LIVING RESORT, TAOS, NEW MEXICO

MAKES 8 GENEROUS ½-CUP SERVINGS OF SORBET AND 4 DOZEN COOKIES

In 2004, De La Tierra was voted one of the world's best new restaurants by the readers of *Conde Nast Traveler* magazine. The management has a commitment to ecological preservation and sustainability—and eating the fruit of the native prickly pear cactus is true to this mission. Rachel Brown, the pastry chef at De La Tierra, devised this deep garnet-colored sorbet. You can make the prickly pear puree in the summer or fall when the cactus fruit is ripe by gathering the fruit with tongs, boiling them for a few minutes, quartering, whirling in the blender, and straining out the seeds and stickers. Use right away or freeze for later use. Use very fine, not stone-ground, cornmeal or your cookies will be gritty. Served in martini glasses or other delicate glassware, this makes for a stunningly elegant dessert. If you don't have an ice-cream maker, freeze the mixture in a bowl until it's almost frozen. Remove from the freezer and beat with an electric mixer. Return it to the freezer. The sorbet will not have as light a texture made this way, but the flavor is still excellent.

PRICKLY PEAR SORBET

¼ cup Madeira

¾ cup sugar

4 cups prickly pear puree (see recipe introduction and Resources)

CORNMEAL–LIME COOKIES
2¼ cups all-purpose flour
¾ cup cornmeal
1 cup sugar
1 teaspoon lime zest
1 cup (2 sticks) plus 5 tablespoons butter
2 egg yolks

A few organic multicolored rose petals, or other nontoxic flower petals, for garnish

FOR THE PRICKLY PEAR SORBET, bring the Madeira and sugar to a simmer over medium-low heat. When the sugar is dissolved, remove it from heat and stir in the prickly pear puree. Let cool, then freeze according to directions for your ice-cream maker (see recipe introduction).

FOR THE CORNMEAL–LIME COOKIES, combine the flour, cornmeal, sugar, and zest in a large bowl. Add the butter and yolks, and work into a dough with your hands until it is soft and tacky. Let the dough rest for 1 hour.

PREHEAT THE OVEN to 350 degrees F. Scoop dough out using a small ice-cream scoop or a large spoon, and roll each scoop into balls about the size of a walnut; place them on a cookie sheet. Bake at 350 degrees F for about 15 minutes or until lightly brown on the bottoms.

TO SERVE, scoop the sorbet into chilled martini glasses. To make chiffonade of rose petals, stack the petals and roll them into a tight tube, like a cigar. Using a sharp knife, make very thin slices, then fluff. Garnish each sorbet with chiffonade of rose petals and a cornmeal lime cookie.

pumpkin flan

RANCHO DE CHIMAYO, CHIMAYO, NEW MEXICO
MAKES 8–10 SERVINGS

The small northern New Mexico town of Chimayo is named for the Tewa Indian word for the red flaking stone in the surrounding hills. Rancho de Chimayo was settled by the Jaramillo family in 1601. In 1965, family members converted one of the original ranch houses into the restaurant. Diners who want to have a leisurely dinner and not worry about driving afterwards can rent a room across the road in another of the restored ranch houses. This recipe calls for making individual servings in small ramekins. If you don't have ramekins, you can bake the custard in any small, oven-proof dishes. This is a good make-ahead dish because it improves in flavor and texture after several hours. It is good on day two as well, but its flavor begins to fade.

CUSTARD
1 fresh pumpkin (2 pounds), or 1½ cups canned pumpkin puree
1 can (17 ounces) evaporated milk
5 eggs
1½ cups sugar
¼ cup dark rum, such as Myers
¾ teaspoon cinnamon
¾ teaspoon ground ginger
⅛ teaspoon ground nutmeg

CARAMEL
2 tablespoons sugar

GARNISH
2 tablespoons piñon nuts, lightly toasted

TO PREPARE THE CUSTARD: If you are using fresh pumpkin, preheat the oven to 350 degrees F. Rinse the pumpkin and cut it in half crosswise. Remove strings and seeds. Place the pumpkin halves on a baking sheet, cut sides down, and bake 45 minutes or more until they are very tender. Remove them from the oven and allow to cool. When cool enough to handle, scrape the pulp from the skin and force the pulp through a ricer or strainer. Measure 1½ cups of the puree, saving the rest for another use. Reduce oven temperature to 300 degrees F.

PLACE ALL OF THE CUSTARD INGREDIENTS into the top of a double boiler, but do not yet move to heat. Whisk steadily for about 1 minute, or until the mixture is well blended and begins to froth at its rim. Insert the pan over its water bath over medium-low heat, and cook until it is warm throughout. Do not let the custard boil. Keep the custard warm in its double boiler over very low heat while preparing the caramel.

TO PREPARE THE CARAMEL: Arrange 8–10 small (½-cup) ramekins or small ovenproof bowls in a shallow pan and place on a counter within easy reach of the stove. Have a padded kitchen mitt nearby for use when it is time to pour the caramelized sugar into the cups.

MEASURE THE SUGAR into a heavy saucepan or skillet, no larger than 1 quart. Cook over low heat, watching carefully as the sugar melts into a golden-brown caramel syrup. (At first, it will seem like nothing is happening, and then it begins to melt very quickly.) There is no need to stir unless the sugar is melting unevenly. When the syrup turns a rich medium-brown, don the padded mitt and immediately remove the pan from the heat, using extreme caution. Pour about ½ teaspoon of caramel into the bottom of each ramekin, continuing to exercise care but moving quickly so the caramel doesn't harden in the pan. The syrup in the bottom of each cup will harden almost immediately. (The quantity of sugar used here, however, does allow a little extra in case some of it hardens in the pan before you can fill all of the cups.)

TO MAKE CLEANING EASIER, place the pan used for liquefying the sugar into a sink and run water in it at once. Stay clear of the hot steam that will rise as the water hits the hot metal surface.

ASSEMBLING THE FLAN: Pour the warmed custard mixture equally into the ramekins on top of the hardened caramel. Add warm water to the pan containing the ramekins or cups, enough to cover the bottom third of the cups. Bake 1 hour and 50 minutes or until the custard is lightly firm and has risen slightly.

REMOVE THE RAMEKINS from the oven in their water bath and let them cool 15–20 minutes at room temperature. Take them out of the pan, cover, and refrigerate for at least 3 hours or overnight.

JUST PRIOR TO SERVING, take the ramekins from the refrigerator and uncover them. Unmold the first dessert by running a knife between the custard and the cup. Cover the cup with an individual serving plate and invert, giving the cup a brief shake to loosen. The custard should drop to the plate, caramel side up. If not, try the process again. Repeat for the remaining custards and serve. Top each portion of flan with a sprinkling of the piñon nuts and serve.

velvet moussellini

VELVET ELVIS PIZZA COMPANY, PATAGONIA, ARIZONA

MAKES 8–10 SERVINGS

The Velvet Elvis in tiny Patagonia has been named by the state's Governor Janet Napolitano as an "Arizona Treasure." Try this dessert—liqueured ice cream served in a wine glass, topped with chocolate cognac sauce and brandy cherries—and you'll agree. According to chef/owner Cecilia San Miguel, this is the most decadent dessert at the Velvet Elvis—and the most popular. You may adjust the amount of the liqueurs in the ice cream to your taste. If you can't find Morella cherries, substitute canned dark cherries. It's best to use high quality vanilla ice cream as your base.

ICE CREAM
½ gallon vanilla ice cream
¼ cup Kahlúa, or other coffee liqueur
¼ cup brandy
⅛ cup rum

CHOCOLATE–COGNAC SAUCE
1½ cups whipping cream
1½ cups semi-sweet chocolate chips
3 tablespoons cognac

BRANDIED CHERRIES
24-ounce jar of Morella cherries in light syrup (see recipe introduction)
4 tablespoons sugar

2 tablespoons yarrow root, or 1½ tablespoons cornstarch
3 tablespoons brandy

TRANSFER THE VANILLA ICE CREAM to a large bowl and allow it to soften enough to whip with a mixer, but do not let it melt entirely. Add the liqueurs and whip until well mixed. Pour the mixture into wine glasses, filling them just ¾ full. Freeze overnight.

FOR THE CHOCOLATE SAUCE, in a saucepan combine the whipping cream and chocolate chips; bring to a boil over medium heat, stirring constantly until the chocolate melts. Remove from heat and whisk until silky smooth. Wisk in the cognac, then let the mixture cool. Top the ice cream-filled glasses with cooled sauce and return to the freezer. Allow the chocolate to set for at least 30 minutes before serving.

FOR THE BRANDIED CHERRIES, strain out the syrup that the cherries come in, then combine it with sugar and yarrow root in a saucepan; bring to a boil over medium heat, stirring constantly. (If you use cornstarch, mix it with a little of the cold cherry syrup first.) Reduce heat and simmer for 10 minutes until thickened. Remove from heat and stir in the brandy and cherries. Refrigerate until ready to serve.

TO SERVE, remove the desserts from freezer and allow to remain at room temperature for 5–8 minutes. Top each glass with a generous portion of chilled brandied cherries.

white chocolate mousse with berries

HEARTLINE CAFÉ, SEDONA, ARIZONA
MAKES 10 SERVINGS

At the romantic Heartline Café, they use an oval-shaped ice cream scoop to portion this mousse onto dessert plates spread with an undersauce of pureed berries. Then they drizzle dark chocolate sauce over the top and garnish with fresh mint and lavender blossoms. Beautiful!

½ cup vanilla ice cream
½ cup butter
2 tablespoons vanilla extract
2 tablespoons Gran Marnier, or other orange liqueur
½ pound white chocolate
1 pint heavy cream
1 egg white, whipped

GARNISH
2 cups raspberries (fresh or frozen)
¾ cup prepared chocolate sauce
10 fresh mint sprigs (optional)
10 lavender flowers (optional)

FOR THE MOUSSE, combine the ice cream, butter, vanilla extract, and Gran Marnier in a small saucepan. Cook over low heat, stirring frequently, until the butter is melted and all ingredients are well mixed. The consistency should be of a thin sauce.

MEANWHILE, melt the white chocolate in a double boiler over medium heat. Stir frequently to maintain a smooth consistency.

USING A MIXER, whip the cream to soft peaks. Do not over-beat. Clean the beaters, and in another bowl whip the egg white until it can hold a stiff peak.

REMOVE THE ICE CREAM MIXTURE and chocolate from the stove. Fold the ice cream mixture into the chocolate, slowly. The secret to this recipe is the slow fold! Add the egg white and continue to fold all ingredients until mixed well. Finally, fold in the whipped cream. Continue to fold until the mixture is consistent and smooth. Chill for at least 2 hours.

FOR THE GARNISH, puree the berries in a blender until very smooth. Strain through a wire sieve. To serve, put a little of the raspberry sauce on a plate and tilt to cover. Top with a scoop of the mousse, a drizzle of chocolate, and the mint and lavender.

caramelized lemon tart

SOLEIL, TUCSON, ARIZONA
MAKES 4 INDIVIDUAL TARTS OR 1 LARGER (10-INCH) TART

Soleil means "sun" in French, and the dining room of this elegant restaurant in the Tucson foothills is drenched with sun during the day. At night it looks out over the sparkling lights of the city. This tart also looks like a big, golden sun. Soleil pastry chef Dorothy D'Alessandro developed the recipe, making good use of the lemons that grow abundantly in southern Arizona and California.

CRUST
4 pre-baked 3½-inch tart shells or a single 10-inch pie shell

LEMON CURD FILLING
Juice of 3 medium lemons
⅔ cup sugar
3 egg yolks
3 whole eggs
¾ cup (1½ sticks) unsalted butter, cut into small pieces
2–3 tablespoons sugar

COMBINE THE LEMON JUICE, sugar, egg yolks, and whole eggs in a medium bowl and whisk until smooth. Cook in the top of a double boiler over medium heat, stirring continuously with a whisk until thickened. While the mixture is still warm, whisk in the butter. Cover and chill overnight.

ASSEMBLE THE TART by spreading the curd evenly with the top of the shell. Sprinkle a thin, even layer of granulated sugar over the top and caramelize with a torch. Or put it under a hot broiler for just 20–40 seconds. Watch it very closely!

beverages

arizona icicle

BISTRO ZIN, TUCSON, ARIZONA

MAKES 1 DRINK

"Hip" and "cool" are the most frequent adjectives applied to the popular Bistro Zin, a restaurant and gathering place on Tucson's northwest side. In fact it's so hip, you might have to wait for a table. Sipping an Arizona Icicle while watching the scene will make the time pass quickly.

2 ounces gin
½ ounce white crème de menthe
½ ounce sambuca

MIX ALL INGREDIENTS over ice in a shaker, then strain and serve in a martini glass.

the pueblo bonito margarita

PUEBLO BONITO BED AND BREAKFAST INN, SANTA FE, NEW MEXICO

MAKES 5–6 DRINKS

Serious tequila drinkers prefer to sip it straight with a wedge of lime on the side. These margaritas, served nightly at the Pueblo Bonito B&B Inn, provide the same flavor. They are very simple to make and differ from the classic margarita in that they do not include triple sec. You can read more about tequila on page 135. Put the lime juice in your freezer forty-five minutes before you want to serve the margaritas so it can freeze to slush. Chilling the punch bowl will help keep the finished margaritas cold.

10 ounces lime juice, frozen to a slushy consistency
5 ounces white (also called silver or blanco) tequila
5 ounces water

1½ cups crushed ice
1 lime, thinly sliced
Margarita salt

POUR THE SLUSHY LIME JUICE, tequila, and water into a blender. Blend well. Take a chilled glass punch bowl from refrigerator and pour the mixture into it. Generously add ice and lime slices. Salt the rims of highball or margarita glasses by rubbing a dampened paper towel over the rims of the glasses, then dipping the glass rims in the margarita salt. Set the glasses around the punch bowl and allow your guests to serve themselves. Don't forget the ladle!

rosalita

DRAGON ROOM BAR, THE PINK ADOBE, SANTA FE, NEW MEXICO
MAKES 1 DRINK

The Dragon Room is considered by many to be the top bar in Santa Fe, and in fact a few years ago the international edition of *Newsweek* named it one of the top twenty bars in the world. It was established in 1977 when the Pink Adobe patio was covered and builders left a tree growing through the roof. (The roof is gone, but the tree is still there!) The drink is a take on a margarita and named for Pink Adobe founder Rosalea Murphy. At the Pink Adobe, bartenders use Jose Cuervo tequila, but any gold tequila will do. If you wish, you can rub the rim of the glass with a piece of lime and then dip it in a saucer of coarse salt.

1½ ounces gold tequila
¾ ounce triple sec
1½ ounces cranberry juice
½ ounce fresh lime juice
Ice
Coarse salt (optional)
¼ ounce Grand Marnier
2 slices lime

SHAKE ALL INGREDIENTS except Grand Marnier, lime slices, and salt together with ice. If desired, rub the rim of a 10-ounce highball glass with one of the lime slices, then dip the rim in coarse salt. Pour the tequila mixture into the prepared glass. Float Grand Marnier on top, then squeeze the remaining lime slice over it.

bloody maria

COPPER QUEEN HOTEL, BISBEE, ARIZONA

MAKES 1 DRINK

The Copper Queen Hotel sits at the heart of the little town of Bisbee and bills itself as the oldest continuously operated hotel in Arizona. There's no better people-watching spot than the front terrace of the Copper Queen. When mining operations closed down, Bisbee reinvented itself as an artists' colony and tourist haven. Heath Brock, a native of Bisbee, is the bartender at the Copper Queen Saloon and makes this Southwestern take on the Bloody Mary.

1 ounce tequila

4–5 dashes of Worcestershire sauce

3–4 shakes celery salt

3–4 shakes pepper

3–4 shakes lemon salt

½ teaspoon horseradish

2 ounces dark beer

4 ounces tomato juice

GARNISH

Lemon and lime slices

SHAKE ALL INGREDIENTS until well blended. Serve in highball glasses over ice and garnish with lemon and lime slices.

the missionary

LA MISIÓN DE SAN MIGUEL, PATAGONIA, ARIZONA

MAKES 1 DRINK

From the exterior, La Misión looks like an old Spanish Colonial church that's been converted to a bar. In fact, it's a ninety-year-old bar that has been given a total makeover inside and out. Owner Cecilia San Miguel, a dreamer with entrepreneurial zeal, oversaw the transformation and now hosts happy customers who come to dance and socialize. There are fewer than a thousand inhabitants of Patagonia itself, but weekends see a busy crowd from the surrounding areas as La Misión offers the only nightlife for miles around. This is the house drink. Tuaca is an orange-vanilla liqueur from Italy.

½ shot Kahlúa
½ shot brandy
½ shot Tuaca
Hot coffee
Whipped cream
Cocoa powder (for garnish)

INTO A GLASS MUG, pour the Kahlúa, brandy, and Tuaca. Fill the remainder of the mug with hot coffee. Stir to mix. Top with whipped cream and sprinkle with cocoa.

DESERT PICNIC

· ·

The Southwest abounds with wonderful destinations for enjoying historical and natural sites, but because distances between places are often far, an excursion might take all day. And some of the most enticing ruins and hiking spots are in remote locations with no nearby restaurants.

The answer to the midday munchies? Pack a delicious picnic full of flavors that define the region. Take a break to eat surrounded by the beauty you have traveled to experience, unhindered by roof or walls. Everything in this suggested menu is sturdy enough to hold up during transport and can be made a day ahead so you can pack up and go in the morning. And if you decide to choose a wine from one of the Southwest's wineries (see page 241), you might want to plan time for a little nap in the sun after lunch.

Here is a suggested menu with recipes from these pages:

APPETIZERS

PUEBLO BONITO GUACAMOLE, PAGE 65

TERRA COTTA SALSA FRESCA, PAGE 211

CORN CHIPS

SALADS (CHOOSE 1–3)

BLACK BEAN SALAD, PAGE 109

SOUTHWEST ROASTED PEPPER AND AVOCADO SALAD, PAGE 113

BROCCOLI–MUSHROOM SALAD, PAGE 110

APPLE CURRY SALAD, PAGE 107

GREEN-APPLE–CELERY-ROOT SLAW, PAGE 115

MAIN DISH AND SIDE

TEQUILA AND CITRUS-GRILLED CHICKEN, SERVED COLD, PAGE 133

JALAPEÑO–BLUE CORN MUFFINS, PAGE 47

DESSERT

PUMPKIN FLAN (BAKE IN ONE CASSEROLE DISH), PAGE 226

FRESH FRUIT

deseo mojito

DESEO, WESTIN KIERLAND RESORT & SPA, SCOTTSDALE, ARIZONA
MAKES 1 DRINK

Deseo ("desire" in Spanish) is an offbeat Nuevo Latino restaurant within the Westin Kierland Resort & Spa. A Mojito is the perfect drink for cooling off after a warm afternoon in the Valley of the Sun. But do be careful—Mojitos go down very smoothly! Vigorous shaking with a few ice cubes bruises the mint leaves and releases their flavor. Unless you have a very well-stocked bar, you probably won't have fresh sugarcane juice or the peeled and sliced sugarcane straws used for garnish at Deseo, but the drink is just as good without.

¼ cup fresh sugarcane juice, or 1 teaspoon sugar
1½ ounces light rum
4–5 fresh mint leaves
Crushed ice
7-Up to taste
1 stick sugarcane for garnish (optional)
1 slice lime for garnish

PLACE THE SUGARCANE JUICE (or sugar), rum, mint leaves, and a little ice in a cocktail shaker and shake vigorously until the sugar dissolves.

FILL A TALL ROCKS GLASS with crushed ice and pour the cocktail over the ice. Add the 7-Up and stir gently. Garnish with the sugarcane stick and lime slice and serve.

WINERIES AND VINEYARDS IN THE SOUTHWEST

Tucked away on back roads, in canyons, and on hillsides all over the Southwest are vineyards growing grapes from stock that originated in Italy, France, Portugal, Spain, and other European countries. Local winemakers are turning out interesting and award-winning vintages that are served in top restaurants, in the homes of savvy wine-lovers, and even at the White House.

The Southwest's high desert areas, with their warm, dry days and cool nights, are perfect for grape growing. In fact, about 80 percent of American native grape varieties grow in Texas.

Wine-grape growing in the Southwest began as early as 1629, when a Franciscan priest and a Capuchin monk planted grapes in Senucu, a pueblo south of Socorro, New Mexico. The priests used the mission variety of grapes to make sacramental wine for the Spanish Colonial churches. By the 1880s, wine was a leading export of the area, and in 1884, New Mexican vintners produced a million gallons of wine.

The situation was similar in Texas. Franciscan padres first planted wine grapes in the El Paso area in 1662, and by the early 1900s, Texas boasted more than twenty commercial wineries. Then came Prohibition in the 1920s, causing wine-making operations all over the country to shut down. The vineyards were abandoned or turned over to other crops.

By the 1970s, Americans were getting interested in wine again, and small winemakers began to respond to the demand, experimenting with various stocks, finding out which ones worked best in their soils and could withstand the summer heat.

Gordon Dutt, a soil specialist and professor at the University of Arizona in the 1970s, was working on a grant to find new agricultural lands and products that would grow in Arizona's climate. He found what he was looking for in an area in the Sonoita Valley, about fifty miles south of Tucson. The climate was right and the soil was surprisingly similar to that of the best wine-growing regions of Burgundy, France. It is called *terra rosa*—red earth—loamy and acidic on the surface, with red clay beneath and a rich layer of lime on the bottom.

Twenty-five years later, Dutt founded Sonoita Vineyards and has been joined by several other winemakers both in the Sonoita Valley and to the east in Cochise County. One of his recent developments is a variety called Arizona

Angel Wings, made from the original mission grapes grown by Spanish priests. The wine is ruby red, very sweet, and, Dutt says, "great for communion wine."

Meanwhile, winemaking has been revived in New Mexico and Texas, too, with every year seeing new plantings and new winemakers. Large commercial vineyards are found in the western part of Texas, with more than fifty wineries producing award-winning wines and making it now the fifth-largest wine-producing state. In a Texas-French Wine Shootout in 2002, wines from Texas and Bordeaux, France, competed in blind taste-tests. Texas won in five of the six categories.

In New Mexico, the resurgence has been in small boutique wineries, about two dozen of them, each with its own specialty. For example, Ponderosa Winery, located in the Jemez Mountains in the north-central part of the state, contends with below-freezing winters. They grow Riesling grapes that produce well in a climate that is similar to Germany. The slightly sweet wines from these grapes can stand up well with New Mexico's spicy foods. Gruet, a vineyard in Albuquerque, is the third-largest producer of sparkling wine in the country—and, according to New Yorker magazine, the best. New Mexican winemakers also produce oak-aged fruit wines, while Bee's Brothers makes honey wine—and, not surprisingly, you can even find chile wine.

Colorado also had an early start to its wine industry. The late 1800s saw growers beginning to plant in the high river valleys east of Grand Junction, and today they are back. At 4,000 to 7,000 feet of elevation, these are the highest vineyards in the world and present a challenge to the growers. However, winemakers feel that the product is worth the effort. The long, warm summer days of intense high-altitude sunlight helps build the natural sugars in the grapes, while the cool mountain evenings allow the grapes to retain the important acids.

Even southern Utah has a few wineries. Of particular interest is a very small company called Native Wines in Mt. Pleasant, northeast of Moab, where proprietors Bob Sorenson and Winnie Wood hand-make twenty-six organic wines, including pear, blackberry, rosehip, and apple, all from fruits picked in the wild.

prickly pear lemonade

EL CORRAL, TUCSON, ARIZONA
MAKES 1 DRINK

El Corral is casual, comfortable, and welcoming. It's the way things were when Tucson was a town, not a city. No attitude here. They specialize in steaks that are thick, juicy, and tender. If you have to wait in the bar for a table to open up, sipping this drink is a good way to pass the time.

1 ounce Captain Morgan Spiced Rum
6 ounces (⅔ cup) lemonade
Splash of prickly pear syrup (see Resources)
Crushed ice

SHAKE ALL INGREDIENTS together and serve in a highball glass.

prickly pear drop

MOSAIC, SCOTTSDALE, ARIZONA
MAKES 1 DRINK

Stephanie Kozicki, the bartender at the Mosaic, developed this drink so that its color matches the blaze of a perfect Arizona sunset. You can make the puree yourself by parboiling prickly pears when they are in season in the summer and early fall, quartering and whirling them in the blender, then straining out the seeds and skins. The puree can be frozen. (You can also order the puree on the Web; see Resources.) You'll find red sugar in the baking section of the grocery store with the cake-decorating supplies.

2 ounces Stoli Strasberi vodka
1 ounce Cointreau
3 teaspoons prickly pear puree (see recipe introduction)
2 lime wedges

Red colored sugar
Twist of lemon

COMBINE VODKA, Cointreau, and prickly pear puree in a martini shaker with ice and shake. Run a lime wedge around the edge of a martini glass and dip in colored sugar. Strain the cocktail into the glass and garnish with the remaining lime wedge and twist of lemon.

chocolate iguana

CHOCOLATE IGUANA, TUCSON, ARIZONA
MAKES 1 SERVING

The original Chocolate Iguana sits on a corner in the heart of Tucson's historic Fourth Avenue Shopping District, and any sunny day finds its outdoor tables full. It started years ago as a small candy shop, a school project for a University of Arizona business student. Over time, it has grown with expanded offerings of coffee, other beverages, and baked goodies of all kinds. Present owner Marci Conklin runs it with the help of her three daughters, Courtney, Aleya, and Chloe. This non-alcoholic treat is their signature offering.

2 shots hot espresso
12 ounces chocolate milk
1 scoop mint chocolate chip ice cream
½ cup whipped cream
1 tablespoon prepared chocolate sauce

IN A 20-OUNCE GLASS, combine the espresso and chocolate milk. Add the ice cream and top with the whipped cream, swirling the chocolate sauce on the top.

iguana italian fresca

CHOCOLATE IGUANA, TUCSON, ARIZONA

MAKES 1 SERVING

Owner Marci Conklin and her daughters had worked for Chocolate Iguana for several years before the small sweet shop went up for sale in the summer of 1999. Since then, this woman-owned and -run business has worked hard to be responsive to its customers. When one woman was longing for a favorite drink, Marci worked to develop this Italian Fresca for her. Marci found she loved it so much that she cannot go a day without one herself. If your grocer doesn't sell Torani syrup, check a specialty store. Non-alcoholic.

Crushed ice
10 ounces club soda
1½ ounces vanilla Torani syrup
1½ ounces half-and-half
1 shot hot espresso
2 tablespoons whipped cream

COMBINE ALL INGREDIENTS except for whipped cream in a 20-ounce glass. Stir very lightly (rapid stirring would release too many bubbles). Top with more ice and a dollop of whipped cream.

watermelon virgin daiquiri

MOSAIC, SCOTTSDALE, ARIZONA

MAKES 1 DRINK

If you are not drinking alcohol, you don't need to feel left out or stuck with a Shirley Temple at the bar at Mosaic, a restaurant that chef/owner Deborah Knight has designed for "the sophisticated yet casual lifestyle of twenty-first-century Arizona." Bartender Stephanie Kozicki developed this stylish and refreshing drink for her teetotaling customers.

¼ cup finely diced watermelon
1 ounce liquid sweet and sour mix
Crushed ice
2 ounces Sprite or 7-Up
Watermelon wedge, about 1 inch across bottom

PICK ANY SEEDS out of the watermelon chunks and blend them very lightly. Add sweet and sour mix and a little crushed ice to the blender and pulse just to combine. Pour into a glass and top with a splash of Sprite or 7-Up and a watermelon wedge.

the restaurants and resorts

Andiamo! Italian Trattoria
322 Garfield Street
Santa Fe, New Mexico 87501
505-995-9595

Anthony's in the Catalinas
6440 North Campbell Avenue
Tucson, Arizona 85718
520-299-1771

Atlas Bistro
2515 North Scottsdale Road
Scottsdale, Arizona 85257
480-990-2433

Big Yellow Inn Bed and
Breakfast
234 South 300 West
Cedar City, Utah 84720
435-586-0960

Bistro Zin
1865 East River Road, Suite 101
Tucson, Arizona 85718
520-299-7799

Brittlebush Bar & Grill
Westin Kierland Resort & Spa
6902 East Greenway Parkway
Scottsdale, Arizona 85254
480-624-1000

Bryce Canyon Lodge
1 Bryce Canyon Road
Bryce Canyon, Utah 84717
435-834-5361

Café Central
109 North Oregon Street
El Paso, Texas 79901
915-545-2233

Café Sonoita
3280 Arizona Highway 82
Sonoita, AZ 85637
520-455-5278

Canyon Ranch
8600 East Rockcliff Road
Tucson, Arizona 85715
520-749-9000

Casa Sedona Bed and Breakfast
Inn
55 Hozoni Drive
Sedona, Arizona 86336
928-282-2938

Chocolate Iguana
500 North Fourth Avenue
Tucson, Arizona 85705
520-798-1211

Christopher's Fermier Brasserie
2584 East Camelback Road
Phoenix, Arizona 85016
602-522-2344

Cien Años
10325 North La Cañada Drive
Oro Valley, Arizona 85737
520-877-8153

Copper Queen Hotel
11 Howell Avenue
Bisbee, Arizona 85603
520-432-2216

Cowboy Club
241 North Highway 89A
Sedona, Arizona 86336
928-282-4200

The Daily Pie Café
Highway 60 MP 56
Pie Town, New Mexico 87827
505-772-2700

De La Tierra
El Monte Sagrado Living Resort
317 Kit Carson Road
Taos, New Mexico 87571
505-758-3502

Deseo
Westin Kierland Resort & Spa
6902 East Greenway Parkway
Scottsdale, Arizona 85254
480-624-1000

El Corral
2201 East River Road
Tucson, Arizona 85718
520-299-6092

Elements at Sanctuary Resort
5700 East McDonald Drive
Paradise Valley, Arizona 85253
480-607-2300

El Monte Sagrado Living Resort
(see De La Tierra, above)

El Tovar Lodge
Grand Canyon National Park
Grand Canyon, Arizona 86023
928-638-2631
888-297-2757 (reservations)

Enchantment Resort (see Yavapai
Restaurant, page 249)

Four and Twenty Blackbirds
620 Old Santa Fe Trail
Santa Fe, New Mexico 87501
505-983-7676

¡Fuego!
6958 East Tanque Verde Road
Tucson, Arizona 85715
520-886-1745

Furnace Creek Inn
Death Valley National Park
Highway 190
Death Valley, California 92328
760-786-2345

Garden Cottage Bed
and Breakfast
16 North 200 West
Cedar City, Utah, 84720
435-586-4919

Ghini's French Caffe
1803 East Prince Road
Tucson, Arizona 85719
520-326-9095

Gold Room at Westward
Look Resort
245 East Ina Road
Tucson, Arizona 85704
520-297-0134

Graze by Jennifer James
3128 Central Avenue SE
Albuquerque, New Mexico 87106
505-268-4729

Heartline Café
1610 West Highway 89A
Sedona Arizona 86336
928-282-0785

Hell's Backbone Grill
20 North Highway 12
Boulder, Utah 84716
435-335-7464

Hilton of Santa Fe
100 Sandoval Street
Santa Fe, New Mexico 87501
505-988-2811

House of Tricks
114 East Seventh Street
Tempe, Arizona 85281
480-968-1114

Inn of the Anasazi
113 Washington Avenue
Santa Fe, New Mexico 87501
505-988-3236

J-Bar
Westin La Paloma Resort
3770 East Sunrise Drive
Tucson, Arizona 85718
520-615-6100

Kai at Sheraton Wild Horse Pass
Resort & Spa
5594 West Wild Horse Pass
Boulevard
Chandler, Arizona 85226
602-458-8000

La Cocina de Luz
123 East Colorado Avenue
Telluride, Colorado 81435
970-728-9355

Lambert's of Taos
309 Paseo del Pueblo Sur
Taos, New Mexico 87571
505-758-1009

La Misión de San Miguel
335 McKeown Avenue
Patagonia, Arizona 85624
520-394-0123

La Posta de Mesilla
2410 Calle de San Albino
Old Mesilla, New Mexico 88046
505-524-3524

Lon's at the Hermosa
5532 North Palo Cristi Road
Paradise Valley, Arizona 85253
602-955-7878

Los Sombreros
2534 North Scottsdale Road
Scottsdale, Arizona 85257
480-994-1799

Maria's New Mexican Kitchen
555 West Cordova Road
Santa Fe, New Mexico 87501
505-983-7929

Medizona
7217 East Fourth Avenue
Scottsdale, Arizona 85251
480-947-9500

Mosaic
10600 East Jomax Road
Scottsdale, Arizona 85262
480-563-9600

North Modern Italian
Restaurant
2995 East Skyline Drive
Tucson, Arizona 85718
520-299-1600

The Palace Bar on Whiskey Row
120 South Montezuma Street
Prescott, Arizona 86303
928-541-1996

Pastiche Modern Eatery
3025 North Campbell Avenue
Tucson, Arizona 85719
520-325-3333

The Phoenician (see *Windows on
the Green, page 249*)

The Pink Adobe
406 Old Santa Fe Trail
Santa Fe, New Mexico 87501
505-983-7712

The Pleasant Street Inn
142 South Pleasant Street
Prescott, Arizona 86303
928-445-4774

Prairie Star Café
288 Prairie Star Road
Santa Ana Pueblo, New Mexico
87004
505-867-3327

Pueblo Bonito Bed and
Breakfast Inn
138 West Manhattan Avenue
Santa Fe, New Mexico 87501
505-984-8001

Rancho de Chimayo
Chimayo, New Mexico 87522
505-351-4444

Remington's
Scottsdale Plaza Resort
7200 North Scottsdale Road
Scottsdale, Arizona 85253
480-948-5000

Roaring Fork
4800 North Scottsdale Road
Scottsdale, Arizona 85251
480-947-0795

Rocking V Café
97 West Center Street
Kanab, Utah 84741
435-644-8001

The Rose Restaurant
234 South Cortez Street
Prescott, Arizona 86303
928-777-8308

Sanctuary Resort (*see Elements,
page 247*)

Scottsdale Plaza Resort (*see
Remington's, above*)

Seven Wives Inn Bed
and Breakfast
217 North 100 West
St. George, Utah 84770
800-600-3737

The Shed
113½ East Palace Avenue
Santa Fe, New Mexico 87501
505-982-9030

Sheraton Wild Horse Pass Resort
& Spa (*see Kai, page 248*)

Simply Delicious Catering
408 East Route 66
Flagstaff, Arizona 86001
928-774-2855

Soleil
3001 East Skyline Drive
Tucson, Arizona 85718
520-299-3345

Sous Chef
1845 East Glenn Street
Tucson, Arizona 85719
520-881-7066

Tall Timber Resort
1 Silverton Star Route
Durango, Colorado 81301
970-259-4813

Terra Cotta
3500 East Sunrise Drive
Tucson, Arizona 85718
520-577-8100

Tonto Bar and Grill
5736 East Rancho Mañana
Boulevard
Cave Creek, Arizona 85331
480-488-0698

Velvet Elvis Pizza Company
292 Naugle Avenue
Patagonia, Arizona 85624
520-394-2102

Waunita Hot Springs Ranch
8007 County Road 887
Gunnison, Colorado 81230
970-641-1266

Westin Kierland Resort & Spa (*see
Brittlebush Bar & Grill, page 247*)

Westin La Paloma Resort (*see
J-Bar, page 248*)

Westward Look Resort (*see Gold
Room, page 248*)

Windows on the Green at the
Phoenician
6000 East Camelback Road
Scottsdale, Arizona 85251
480-941-8200

Yavapai Restaurant
Enchantment Resort
525 Boynton Canyon Road
Sedona, Arizona 86336
928-282-2900

Zion Lodge
Zion National Park
Springdale, Utah 84767
435-772-7700

RESOURCES

The following businesses are good
mail-order sources for certain
Southwest ingredients that you may
want to experiment with but can't
find at your local supermarket.

Atlantic Game Meats
207-862-4217
www.atlanticgamemeats.com
Atlantic is a source for excellent
farm-raised venison steaks.

Bueno Foods
2001 Fourth Street
Albuquerque, NM 87102
800-95-CHILE (800-952-4453)
www.buenofoods.com
Items available at Bueno include
blue cornmeal, fresh New Mexico
green chiles in season, frozen
chopped New Mexico green chiles,
pure ground red chile powders,
and red chile puree.

Canyon Wren Ranch
92425 Aravaipa Road
Winkleman, AZ 85292
520-357-7501
Raises and sells USDA-inspected
and processed grass-fed lamb from
Churro sheep.

Cheri's Desert Harvest
1840 East Winsett
Tucson, AZ 85719
800-743-1141
www.cherisdesertharvest.com
A good place to get prickly pear
syrup; you can call, order from the
website, or request a free catalog.

GourmetSleuth.com
Online source for all Mexican
ingredients including Ibarra
chocolate, dried whole chiles and
chile powders, achiote (annatto) paste and seeds,
Mexican oregano, posole corn,
mole sauces, canned huitlachoche,
and masa harina.

Mexgrocer.com
Many Mexican products are available here, including dried chiles,
achiote (annatto) seeds, blue corn,
masa harina, mole sauces, corn
husks, and Mexican chocolate.

Native Seeds/SEARCH
526 North Fourth Avenue
Tucson, AZ 85705
886-622-5561
www.nativeseeds.org
Another good source to call or

visit the website; you'll find blue
cornmeal, dried beans, whole
dried chiles, red and green chile
powder, posole, and prickly pear
products.

Rivenrock Gardens
www.rivenrock.com
John Dicus carries organically
grown, nearly spineless prickly
pear pads in several grades, all of
which are picked fresh the day
they are shipped—so worth the
price! Ordering is via the website
only.

Santa Cruz Chili and Spice
Company
1868 East Frontage Road
P.O. Box 177
Tumacacori, AZ 85640
www.santacruzchili.com
Like the name says, this is where
you find chile paste, chile
powder, and other chile—and
chili—products.

Shepherd's Lamb
Box 307
Tierra Amarilla, New Mexico
87575
www.organiclamb.com
505-588-7792
Shepherd's certified organic lambs
graze on grass in the New Mexico
mountains; lamb is shipped frozen.

INDEX